The Mystical State
Politics, Gnosis, and Emergent Cultures

The Mystical State:
Politics, Gnosis, and Emergent Cultures

Arthur Versluis

New Cultures Press
Minneapolis, Minnesota

Library of Congress Cataloging-in-Publication Data

Versluis, Arthur, 1959-
 The mystical state : politics, gnosis, and emergent cultures / Arthur Versluis.
   p. cm.
 ISBN-13: 978-1-59650-011-2 (alk. paper)
 ISBN-10: 1-59650-011-5
 1. Mysticism--Political aspects. 2. Gnosticism--Political aspects. 3. Negative theology-
-Christianity--Political aspects. 4. Occultism--Religious aspects--Christianity--Political
aspects. I. Title.
 BV5083.V46 2011
 273'.1--dc22

                          2010044723

                    Text set in Minion Pro
EPub ISBN: 978-159650-012-9
                  Copyright © 2011 Arthur Versluis

        The paper used in this publication meets the minimum requirements of ANSI/NISO
Z39.48-1992 (R 1997) (Permanence of Paper).

                    New Cultures Press
                  Minneapolis, Minnesota

                      Visit us at
                  www.newcultures.org

Printed and bound in the United States of America.

15 14 13 12 11   1 2 3 4 5 6 7 8 9 10

Different versions of chapters of this book were previously published in the
following scholarly journals: *Studies in Spirituality*, *Telos*, and *Temenos Academy
Review*. Our thanks to their editors, publishers, and peer reviewers.

Contents

Introduction

This is not just another book—for it opens a new way of seeing the world and our way of being in it. In it, we look back at the history of the West and see it in a new light. It is not only retrospective, nor does it offer a pessimistic view of the future, though we must look clearly and without illusions at the nature of our era. At heart, *The Mystical State* looks toward the future, toward what is possible on the other side of the difficult times that undoubtedly still lie ahead. *The Mystical State* is a book that looks much deeper into the origins of modernity than has been done before, and it looks toward how we can create new cultures, new ways of being in the world that are not homicidal or ecocidal, but humane, and natural. This is possible. The purpose of this book is to point the way.

We must begin, though, by considering what is meant by the term "modernity." Essentially, modernity is an historical category—it begins with "early modernity," a nebulous term denoting perhaps what follows the "medieval era," and proceeds through "the modern age" to the present moment, which is, of course, what "modern" actually means: "present, now, this historical moment." In truth, "modernity's" characteristics—secularity, for instance—we can discern only after distinguishing its historical boundaries that, inevitably, end with our own present moment. We can "place" modernity's beginning earlier or later, as we wish, but we are compelled to see the present as a part of it. Some want to remove "modernity" from its historical situation so as to make room for various speculations, but my point is that it cannot *be* so removed, and for that matter, neither can the fictive "postmodern" remove the weight of historicity. In fact, quite the opposite: "modern," "postmodern," or "aftermodern," whatever, all are inescapably temporal.

The word "culture" also is used blithely, as in "popular culture," or "Hollywood culture" or "corporate culture," the notion apparently being that culture is more or less synonymous with "society," and signifies little more than one or another group ethos. However, this colloquial and modern use of the word ignores its much older and deeper meanings. Culture, after all, is etymologically linked to *cultus*, that is, to the invisibility of labor and worship, a relationship visible in a ritual image or instrument whose cultural significance is imbued by the cult that brought it into being. This point is profoundly important: culture requires *cultus*. There is no culture without *cultus* at its center.

But secular modernity consists in the detachment of culture from *cultus*, something inconceivable in a traditional culture where everything, all implements and clothing, bears the imprint of the sacred. In the same way, a traditional culture's worldview is inconceivable in secular modernity, whose foundational perspective is dualistic, objectifying, commodifying. Hence the corrosive effect secular modernism inexorably has on traditional cultures around the world. Indeed, secular modernity is toxic as a kind of side effect, resulting in the apparently inexorable decline and disappearance of traditional cultures.

During the era often self-designated as "modernity," the political seemed to become ever more prominent in society. Yet the political never provided solutions to the enormous problems generated by modernity itself; rather, it provided a kind of entertainment, a diversion similar to sporting events. One might root for this or that team, this or that contestant, but victory meant primarily the temporary accrual of power to a particular side. And in the contests, no one discussed the central problems intrinsic to modernity itself—if someone did, he thus declared himself to be marginal. The rules of the game were to present oneself as "mainstream," that is, as an iconic manifestation of the system itself, at once "charismatic" and yet a member of the managerial elite. The modern system perpetuated itself with a remarkable lack of reflection or analysis—indeed, one could even say that this lack of reflection is essential to the modern system.

The phrase "modern system," here, is deliberate. "Modernity," an historical category, here is also a shorthand reference to industrial-technological society that, already by the mid-twentieth century, had become hegemonic and that, although certainly not uniform, nonetheless was global in scope. A primary means of this global hegemony was, of course, technology. Technology, once introduced, becomes mandatory—necessary simply to function in modern society. One can hardly hold a job or even undertake a task if one refuses to employ the technology necessary to perform it. But with this technology, modernity consumes: seemingly inexorably, it converts everything that can be consumed into products that in fact *are* consumed. In particular, it consumes nature, and it absorbs and destroys traditional cultures.

How did secular modernity come to be? In order to understand our own era, we have to look much further back in history, at its ancient sources. Central to our subject is the theme of gnosis, which is the pivot upon which culture turns. Gnosis refers to the unifying spiritual knowledge at the center of a culture, linking together the three realms of humanity, nature, and the divine. To put it another way, gnosis is the hidden crystalline filament woven through and illuminating a living culture. Its absence can manifest in a variety of ways, and one of those is secular modernity, where all three realms are separated from one another.

That "gnosis" and "gnosticism" are polemical categories is clear. Ever since late antiquity, the category "gnosis" has taken on a pejorative cast, and has been relegated to the larger category of "heresy." The harsh anti-heretical rhetoric and accusations of Tertullian, Irenaeus, and Epiphanius, who attacked and ridiculed the very notion of "gnosis," were instrumental in establishing the fundamental parameters of what was considered acceptably within the category of "orthodox," and those parameters remained largely definitive up to the present day. Nineteenth and twentieth-century scholarship concerning "gnosis" and "Gnosticism" largely repeated heresiophobic typologies carried over almost intact from late antiquity, so that "gnosis" remained suspect, as did the very notion of "transcendence."

But as the discoveries of actual Gnostic texts from late antiquity became available, many scholars of Gnosticism became increasingly uneasy with characterizations of "Gnosticism," and one prominent scholar went so far as to observe that "the variety of phenomena classified as 'Gnostic' simply will not support a single, monolithic definition, and in fact *none of the primary materials fits the standard typological definition*."[1] For years, scholars called into question the stereotypical notions of "Gnosticism," like the cliché that Gnosticism was "a radically dualistic, anti-cosmic tradition capable of producing only two extreme ethical possibilities: either an ascetic avoidance of any fleshly or worldly contamination (often caricatured as hatred of the body and the world) or a depraved libertinism that mocks any standards of moral behavior."[2] The Nag Hammadi texts (a collection of Gnostic treatises discovered in the mid-twentieth century) did not confirm these clichés, but instead revealed a spectrum of cosmological and ethical perspectives—and not one treatise confirmed the heresiophobes' accusations of Gnostic "anti-cosmic" "dualist" "libertinism."

In fact, the more I studied the phenomena grouped under the heading of "Gnostic," or for that matter, under headings like "mystic," the more dubious I became about most ancient or contemporary depictions or interpretations of them. When one reads the Gospel of Thomas, for instance, one is struck by the lapidary power of its aphorisms, and is compelled by original sources like this to doubt that the fulminations of Tertullian were valid, and that scholars like Hans Jonas are describing anything other than their own existentialist philosophy. My close study of Christian theosophy of the early modern era revealed the same kinds of disconnects between the actual works and what many had written about them. Books like *Wisdom's Children* and *Wisdom's Book* represented my efforts to reveal Christian theosophy not as misguided "heresy" but as the theosophers themselves understood it.

My doubts were intensified about "heresiography" as I examined and then wrote about the long Western history of heretic-hunting in an earlier book, *The New Inquisitions*, for in the process of researching and writing it, I realized just how deeply ingrained in the West is the syndrome of scapegoating "heretics." Here is a class of phenomena integral to the emergence of much intellectual or ideological architecture that we mostly still take for granted today, and not only in Christianity. But in Christianity first and primarily, anti-gnosticism and anti-mysticism resulted in the emphasis upon religious belief or faith rather than on religious knowledge; the emphasis on history and time, rather than on transcendence or timelessness, closely linked to teleological or eschatological interpretations of history.

Slowly I came to realize that, far from belonging only to a mostly-forgotten and distant era of late antiquity, questions concerning "heresy" and "orthodoxy," "gnosis" and "anti-gnosis" are of great importance if we are to more clearly understand what we may call the intellectual substructure of our own time. Here I am not referring only to what we may call the "secularization hypothesis," meaning the view that modernity emerged from the secularization of Christian theology and culture. Such a perspective is certainly visible in the work of Max Weber on Protestantism and capitalism, as also in the work of Carl Schmitt on what he termed "political theology," which is allied to Roman Catholicism. There is much to be said for the "secularization hypothesis" as a way of interpreting why and how secular modernity came into existence. Indeed, *The New Inquisitions* traces how the inquisitional phenomenon was transformed from a Roman Catholic context into a semi-secularized and then a militantly secular context in an intellectual lineage that runs from Joseph de Maistre and Juan Donoso Cortés through Georges Sorel into various twentieth-century totalitarian states. But here we are going deeper than the "secularization hypothesis" allows—beyond intellectual history into intellectual archaeology.

Secular modernity, I found, both derives from and reflects a conflict that goes back at least to the period of late antiquity.[3] This conflict has its origins the rejection by those who positioned themselves as orthodox of those who dissented from their more or less strictly historical and confessional version of Christianity. The alternative forms of Christianity during this early period are sometimes described as "Gnostic," meaning that instead of a religion based only on faith, they insisted on the central-ity of gnosis, or direct spiritual insight. The gnostics were relegated to the category of "heresy," during this formative period, and in fact still to this day, mysticism and gnosis are largely excluded both from religious and scientific perspectives, and rarely appear except as derogatory terms.

In fact, some schools of thought during the twentieth century explicitly revived the ancient obloquy directed at the "old enemy" of the Gnostics, blaming them for the problems of the present day.[4] Somehow, accord-ing to these various good haters of gnosis and Gnosticism, perspectives that had been more or less successfully extirpated and repressed dur-ing the period of late antiquity, despite their almost total absence from the conceptual universe of modernity, were held to be responsible for the ills of modernity. Such a claim is hard to fathom. Still, behind this derogatory rhetoric about gnostics was a very real fear. It was the fear of transcendence.[5] In the view of such modern anti-gnostics, modernity is "legitimated" by its rejection of transcendence and gnosis, and its reduc-tion of the conceptual universe to what one can grasp with the hands and little more. From such a perspective, it would appear that what matters is only time and materiality as we conventionally know them: we might call such a viewpoint historism.

But if one reverses this argument, one gets a very different result. Let us posit that modernity indeed reflects to a considerable extent the rejec-tion of gnosis and the Gnostics back in late antiquity—that modernity came into being as the "second rejection" of gnosis. Let us suppose that exactly as anti-Gnostics have suggested, modernity does derive from the rejection of gnosis. Yet in this alternative interpretation, many of the evils of modernity—ecocide and genocide for instance—would be held to come not from gnostics, but from those for whom the very concept of gnosis is totally foreign. Ecocide and genocide take place as a result, not of non-dualistic gnosis informed by loving kindness, but of dualism and a reduction of nature and of others to mere objects. You begin to see the direction of my thinking here.

In this book, we begin to explore this new intellectual territory. In *The New Inquisitions*, we were looking at the worst examples, at the horrors visited upon humanity in the twentieth century, and at what gave rise to those horrors, the most negative examples in human history. But here we will again go back to the origins of Christianity, this time looking at the positive or affirmative dimensions of what the heresiophobes denounced. What are the socio-political implications or ramifications of gnosis or the transcendence of self-other dualism? Surely there are some, after all. But what? Only recently have there been a few intimations in contemporary philosophical and religious thought that we might have much to learn from gnosis, mysticism, or negative theology.[6] And these efforts have been far from systematic or complete.

There are two aspects to such an inquiry, one an engagement in speculative metaphysics, the other historical. These two dimensions are, of course, intertwined. Required is a sustained effort at intellectual reconstruction and engagement in ways that are almost unprecedented, and certainly will be unfamiliar to most of us. Investigating the socio-political and cultural implications of gnosis entails intellectual archaeology on the most profound levels, and a reconsideration of the entire intellectual substrata of the modern industrial period.

For such an inquiry, we may take as our watchwords William Blake's lines from the very beginning of the industrial period:

Both read the Bible day and night
But thou read'st black where I read white
or again
The vision of Christ that thou dost see
Is my vision's greatest enemy.[7]

One cannot expect—given the long history of heretic-hunting in the West over two millennia, let alone the secularization, globalization, and industrialization of heretic-hunting in the twentieth century—that an inquiry like this one will be universally welcomed. But it is nonetheless high time that we undertake it. I hope you enjoy the journey as much as I do.

Chapter One

What is Gnosis?

Few terms are more polysemic than "gnosis" and "Gnosticism." Because these words are charged with millennia of opprobrium, it is now quite difficult to see back through the murky, sediment-laden waters into what, exactly, Gnosticism or gnosis might have meant in the early Christian period. Much contemporary scholarship still derives from the fierce polemics of the early Christian fathers like Tertullian, and so even today one finds relatively widespread assertions that Gnostics were libertines, dualistic, anti-worldly, and so forth. Here, we will not continue this tradition of polemics, but rather will seek to recover what lay at the very heart of Gnosticism, and that is central to our entire project here. Nearly all efforts have been to reconstruct one form or another of Gnosticism—but here we will investigate not Gnosticism, but gnosis, and in particular that of Basilides, who belonged to the second century A.D.

After all, the word *gnosis* by definition precedes and underlies subsequent words like "Gnostic" or "Gnosticism." Yet what does the word *gnosis* mean? It is interesting that here too we find polemics. Whereas there is, especially in the work of Clement of Alexandria, precedent for at least the idea of an authentic gnosis within Christianity, almost nowhere in subsequent Western Christianity does one find this idea taken up. Thus, by the beginning of the twenty-first century, one finds the word *gnosis* still being used pejoratively, as when Catholic theologian Johann Baptist Metz writes that "Christianity does not support any gnostic dualism between time and eternity, between creation and redemption," and rejects any notion of "atemporality of salvation" in favor of a "still-outstanding end of time."[8] He rejects a "world-blind gnosis," which he thinks is characteristic also of "Eastern mysticism" and, for that matter, of Buddhism.[9] But since such a dismissal of Buddhism can only be accomplished by ignoring what Buddhism actually teaches, one has to wonder whether the same might be true of gnosis.

Scholars have long wondered to what degree Buddhism and Gnosticism might have been linked in late antiquity, particularly in the school founded by Basilides, the earliest of the Alexandrian Gnostics (ca. 120 A.D.), and said to be a disciple of St. Matthias and of Glaucias, a disciple of St. Peter. Basilides, as is well known, taught a negative mysticism that is closely akin to the Prajnaparamita Sutra.[10] Both reject the ultimate value of any analogy in understanding the nature of direct spiritual knowledge—it is not like this, or like that. It is not up, or down, black, or white, but in the words of the Prajnaparamita Sutra, echoing the very earliest Buddhist sources, it is "gone-beyond," that is, it is absolute transcendence of all dualistic knowledge. Is it possible that *gnosis* is, at the deepest level, a word that expresses the same kind of non-dualistic, transcendent insight that we see at the heart of Buddhism? According to Hippolytus, Basilides emphasized the sheer and utter transcendence of the divine nature, which is not even conceivable by man.[11]

Basilides held that prior to existence of creation, "nothing existed," "not matter, nor substance, nor what is insubstantial, nor is absolute, nor composite, nor conceivable, nor inconceivable, nor sensible, nor devoid of senses, nor man, nor angel, nor a god, nor any object with a name, or apprehended by sense, or cognized by intellect."[12] Out of this emerged a Will, which brought into being the variegated germ or seed of existence within which were all aspects of being in vitro, as symbolized by the multi-colored peacock's tail. One has to read through or past Hippolytus, however, because any teachings of Basilides are obscured by layers of Hippolytian invective and interpretation. Thus, for instance, the above passages are all read through an opaque lens of "Aristotelianism," since Hippolytus's rhetorical method is to almost indiscriminately attribute the teachings of "heretics" to earlier, almost always unrelated Greek authors and thus to dismiss them. But in fact Basilides' teachings had nothing to do with Aristotle.

Rather, Basilides (it soon becomes clear) taught a complex and fascinating doctrine of emanationism that is constantly informed by an awareness of what we may call Nothingness, transcendence, or, if we wish to use a Buddhist term, emptiness. For instance, from what we can understand as conveyed through the writings of Hippolytus, Basilides described the mysterious relationship between the Holy Spirit and the Son. In order to come into the world of being or existence, the Son had to "leave behind" the Spirit and that "Blessed Place that cannot be conceived or represented by any expression."[13] Thus the Son serves as a vehicle or mode of translation between the realm of form or conceivable, earthly existence, and formlessness or transcendence.

This relationship between above and below can be understood via the Basilidean analogy of "a most fragrant ointment," traces of which remain in a vessel even after the ointment is poured out. Likewise "the Holy Spirit has continued without any share in the Sonship," and yet they mysteriously remain "coterminous." Thus Basilides seeks to convey the profound relationships between absolute transcendence on the one hand and the discrete elements of sensory perception on the other. How did the Son come into existence from absolute transcendence? Emanation or translation, which can only be understood in relation to a "background" of what Basilides calls, in a strikingly Buddhist term, "Formlessness." The analogy of fragrance is ideal for conveying how a phenomenon can exist and yet at the same time, not be graspable—that is, for conveying how formlessness inheres in form.

In other words, Basilides' teachings answered the profound question of how unity or transcendence and multiplicity or immanence can be understood in relation to one another, and of how existence herebelow is related to transcendence. The Son, or "Sonship" (a term that emphasizes the *functional* nature of the Christ as opposed to a discrete historical existence) emanates "downward" into existence—Sonship translates transcendence into immanence, light into darkness. Sonship both receives blessings from above and confers them below. Thus Sonship also serves as the vehicle that "reverses" the fall into discrete, divided, individual identity—Sonship is the vehicle for translation from lower into higher being, a process analogous to the movement of eagle's wings that allow it to soar upward.[14] The Sonship within us strives upward, becoming ever more "refined," because it is "firmly connected with the light that shines down from above."[15] The emanation from above to below (that is, the process of divine emanation and revelation) is implicitly also the promise for humanity of translation from below to above.

The human psyche is central to this process, and so we find a complex psychology attributed to both Basilides and his son Isidore. According to the account of Clement of Alexandria, the foundation of this psychology is that the fallen soul is host to many alien "appendages" or parasitic attachments. These can be understood symbolically as having the forms of animals or plants—for instance, the wolf or the pig, corresponding to ravenous predation or greed. The fallen soul is thus distorted into multiple forms, which represent the psyche as attached to the outer world in various ways. The process of spiritual awakening is thus the process of transcending or pacifying these inner "parasites."[16] Someone whose soul is distorted into such forms and attached to the outward world is by definition in a state of ignorance, whereas the more detached one is, the more free one is from these psychological drivers of anger, fear, greed, envy, and so forth.

As one, through spiritual awakening, pacifies or transcends these "parasites" or inner drivers, one also transmutes the five aspects of the individual into what could be termed the transcendent bodies or "vehicles." Hence, at death the various aspects of the elect dissolve or enter into their various spheres, matter into matter, and so forth up to the realization of the transcendent by that which is transcendent within one. But those who have not undergone a process of spiritual awakening are at death still subject to the drives of these "appendages" or "parasites," and so they reincarnate in some new form according to the forces or karma most dominant within them.[17] After death, then, one either enters into a transcendent "region" according to one's degree of spiritual realization, or one continues on a path of metempsychosis or transmigration and further suffering in ignorance.

Just as the individual comes into existence in the world through the continuation of previous "stored" tendencies, so too does existence as a whole come into being via the collective "germ" or *pan-spermia* of karmic tendencies. Gnosis is the transcendence of this limiting or karmic realm. This "germ" realm, as Basilides called it, is akin to what in Buddhism is called the *alaya-vijnana*, or the repository of preëxisting tendencies, a realm that is "above" physical existence but "below" transcendence. What Basilides calls "Sonship" is the means by which the transcendence of the supernal Spirit is able to illuminate existence from a realm beyond the delimiting sphere of the "germ" or "seed-mass." The revelation of Christ penetrates through the sphere of stored karmic tendencies, but we can cognize that revelation only through faith—that is, through the aspiration to comprehend the incomprehensible, or to cognize what transcends cognition. From the one side of the "germ," a hand reaches down, and from the other, a hand reaches up. When the two meet, that is gnosis.

But it must be kept in mind that for Basilides, gnosis is not describable, because God himself is not explicable or describable in any terms whatever. God is better understood as *ouk on theos*, or "Not-being God:"

> Since "nothing" existed, neither matter nor form, nor accident; neither the simple nor the compound, neither the unknowable nor the invisible, neither man nor angel nor god nor any of these things, which are called by names or perceived by the mind or the senses. The Not-Being God (*ouk on theos*) whom Aristotle calls Thought of thought (*noesis tes noeseos*), without consciousness, without perception, without purpose, without aim, without passion, without desire, had the will to create the world. I say "had the will" only by way of speaking, because in reality he had neither will, nor ideas nor perceptions; and by the word 'world' I do not mean this actual world, which is the outcome of extension and division, but rather the Seed of the world. The seed of the world contained in itself, as a mustard seed, all things which are eventually evolved, as the roots, the branches, the leaves arise out of the seedcorn of the plant.[18]

Basilides insists on the absolute transcendence of apparent subject-object dichotomy of any kind whatever, and in this he is affirming what we also see in the Buddhist Prajnaparamita Sutra, and in the Buddhist tradition as a whole. So important to Basilides and his followers was this emphasis on "Not-being" that they became known as the *oukontiani*, or those who always spoke of the *oukon*, [not-being].

Notably, even in these highly negative accounts of Basilides and his teachings as found in the Church Fathers, we still can discern the main elements of what later would come to be known as "orthodox" or "confessional" Christianity. Basilides apparently composed exegeses of the Gospels; he accepted the historical existence of Christ; he accepted the moral authority of the Old Testament; he accepted the doctrine of the Trinity—the list goes on. What then differentiated Basilides from the "orthodox"? Basilides offered a complete and vast metaphysics; his Christianity enveloped but transcended what came to be known as "orthodoxy" because he included profound philosophical dimensions. One could easily conclude that Basilides represented (in 120 A.D.) a metaphysically complete Christianity that is closely akin to Buddhism; whereas confessional Christianity was a truncated version missing all that we find in Basilides.

It is of course possible to attribute the metaphysics of Basilides to Buddhism, or to the influence of Platonism. Scholars have long wondered what the connections were between Basilides and Buddhism, which after all by 120 A.D. was already well developed and widely dispersed.[19] And there are many elements of Basilides' teachings that remind us of Plato himself as well as of later Platonists, notably Plotinus, but also others. Yet clearly Basilides is Christian—he is obviously and completely a witness to the metaphysical power of the revelation of Christ. Furthermore, he is clearly a witness to the divine *oukon*, or not-being of that revelation. As a witness or participant, as a gnostic or knower, although Basilides may have drawn from Buddhism and Platonism, his realization was both his own and part of an initiatory lineage going back to the apostles of only a generation before.

And so we return again to our central and indispensable question: what is gnosis? In the tradition of Basilides, it is a direct realization, through the aspiration of faith, of the divine power or "not-being" of Christ. For Basilides, Christ penetrates into and "opens" history. Christ is the vertical incision into the otherwise endless horizontal plain of suffering; hence Christ not only lives on earth as man, but also harrows the underworld. He illumines all realms of existence with what can only be described, with an awareness of the insufficiency of the description, as *oukon*. Christ is the revelation to suffering man of the liberating freedom of *not-being*. Realization of that revelation is gnosis.

While affirming gnosis, Basilides does not decry creation as evil. Indeed, quite the opposite. Clement of Alexandria, hardly a Basilidean, acknowledges that Basilides says "I will admit anything, rather than that the divine constitution of the world is evil."[20] We must recognize the importance of such an assertion. Basilides is not condemning the world or history as evil—but he does recognize that the world and its historical unfolding is a vale of tears. To recognize the existence of evil and suffering is not to condemn existence itself, but simply to observe a fact. And thus we can see the injustice of the perspective asserted by Metz who, in rejecting an imagined Gnostic "world-blindness" or "dualism," is only echoing a longstanding series of wrongful accusations that can be traced right back to the era of the Church Fathers and their invectives against Basilides and other Gnostics.

Gnosis, for Basilides, is the absolute transcendence of subject-object duality. As such, it cannot even be said to be selfless, because gnosis is beyond the self-other dichotomy. This is why Basilides' expressions are so artfully constructed, why he seeks to deploy language against its own inherent tendency toward fixed or reified concepts. He writes, for example, "I say, [of God] 'had the will,' only as a manner of speaking," because he knows that the human linguistic tendency is to project a human self onto God, in effect, to reduce God to humanly comprehensible terms. Basilides understood what was also understood by Dionysius the Areopagite, and much later by Jacob Böhme and John Pordage: that experientially the Divine is best expressed in negative terms as "not this and not that," or as what Böhme terms the *ungrund*, the not-ground prior to being or existence, which in turn derives from the *Nichts*, or Divine Nothing, what Eckhart called the Godhead.[21]

Perhaps the reader will allow us to indulge in an hypothesis here. Suppose the extraordinary power of the Christian revelation is inherently at odds with the reifying power of language. The force of the Christian revelation is precisely in its transcendence of the self-other division, but this is inherently in opposition to both the self-other distinctions inherent in language and to the fundamental human tendency to build and cling to conceptual constructs or ideology. Thus from the very beginning, Christianity would have consisted in a struggle between those who were privy to the transcendent gnosis of Christ and the apostles, and those who instead fell prey to the fallen tendency to cling to concepts or ideology as if they were central, not transcendence. Were this so, then one could see why a gnostic like Basilides might be vilified by those whose natural tendency was to cling to self-other distinctions so strongly as to want to kill "heretics." To them, a Basilides and his school represented a constant reproach, a reminder of transcendent gnosis that by its very nature refused worldly power or authority because its kingdom is not of this world.

Gilles Quispel alluded to the implications of this struggle when, only at the very end of his major article on Basilides, he asks "Is this Gnostic God, this mystical God, different from the God of the Bible? Is he another God? This problem is delicate, terrifying in fact."[22] But Quispel does not want to offer an answer to these questions, and we can see why—they are discomforting. However, they also point to what I believe is absolutely central to understanding the nature of the Basilidean gnosis. Basilides' gnosis is non-dualistic, and is expressed in terms of negative theology. It is not expressed in terms of a rejection of the Old Testament, in the manner of Marcion, but in its very nature it is transcendence of dualistic, friend/foe conceptualizations and institutionalizations. Hence it would seem rather obvious that the God of Leviticus and Deuteronomy is not what Basilides is describing.

And so we might begin to see political implications emerging. At this point, it is worth observing that Basilides did not found any enduring institutional structure. He did found an initiatory line to which his son Isidore also belonged. And we know that there were Basilideans extant as late as the fourth and possibly fifth centuries, mostly in Egypt, but also in Italy, Greece and possibly in Spain. But the Basilidean lineage seems to have emphasized praxis and experience over doctrinal rigidity or institutional structure—it was an *approach* to the Christian revelation, not an institutionalization of it. In this, too, it had much in common with the Christian theosophic tradition of Jacob Böhme that begins in the seventeenth century. As a praxis, Basilides reportedly enjoined five years of silence as part of adherents' training; and his line also encouraged the wearing of amulets that were imbued with the "fragrance" or "imprint" of the school's gnostic revelations. But we find no trace of doctrinal coërcion: his school existed within the larger context of Christianity as a revelation of its higher dimensions, and one was free to accept or to ignore it. In this, too, it is quite akin to Buddhism.

Is a negative theology also a negative politics? It would seem so, would it not? That Gnosticism emphasized the inner life over institutional authority is obvious, but perhaps less obvious is that a negative theology—a recognition that language and doctrine are only indicative, not to be clung to and reified—itself has anti-bureaucratic sociopolitical implications. The construction of an institutional hierarchy and its identification with the apparatus of the state, these emerge from what we may term "externalist" theology based in human reason, and on the dualistic premise of a self/other relation between God and man.

By contrast, philosophically, the Basilidean negative theology arguably offers more satisfactory solutions to fundamental intellectual problems precisely because it eschews dualism and embraces a speculative, nuanced, and complex metaphysics that resolves questions like, for instance, how existence emanated out of transcendence. No ponderous and literalistic dualism here. Hence it only makes sense that a Basilidean Gnosticism does not form an enduring institutional bureaucracy, because it also does not lend itself to a dualistic "orthodox/heretic" dualism. Rather, the Basilidean line exists within the context of Christianity as a whole, with which it has no quarrel, and simply offers, to those who wish to pursue it, a gnostic path of realization. Those who do not wish to pursue such a path do not have to.

A negative politics means one's guiding political watchword is that, as Jesus himself commanded, one does not judge others. This does not mean one is undiscerning or lacks judgment. Rather, it means that Christianity is not deployed as the basis of a juridical system, as Tertullian and the majority of the Ante-Nicene Fathers sought to do. A negative politics means that one is discerning, but one does not seek to impose one's understanding upon others—one concentrates on the beam in one's own eye, not on the mote in someone else's. A negative theology translates, on a human level, into a refusal to hunt for heretics, a refusal to employ the apparatus of the state or the church in the service of ideological or doctrinal constructs. Why? Because negative theology, in its very nature, requires awareness of the fundamental inadequacy and the mere instrumentality of language and concepts.

I have chosen to concentrate on Basilides here, both because he is relatively early (within a generation or two of Christ and the apostles), and because we can discern in his teachings and lineage so much that is visible elsewhere in the history of Christianity. His example is synecdochic—he represents and in many respects incarnated what was excluded by the Ante-Nicene Fathers, by Augustine, and by the emergence of an "orthodoxy" that could bolster its legitimacy primarily by dualistic rejection, that is, by projecting "heresy" onto Basilides, his followers, and countless other Gnostic groups and individuals. It is true that later, negative theology crept back into "orthodoxy" via the back door represented by the writings of Dionysius the Areopagite. But the relationship of negative theology with "orthodoxy" remained vexed, right up to the present.

In order to understand the implications of negative theology, we need to turn first to exoterism, to the outward rather than the inward dimensions of what are often termed the Abrahamic traditions. The dynamic that informs the monotheistic religious traditions is quite influential today, not only in the religious traditions themselves, but also more broadly in secular or semi-secular society. By exploring what I am terming here the legacy of monotheism, we are better able to recognize how it operates, as well as what alternatives there are. An exoteric/esoteric opposition is not necessary—one does not find such an oppositional dynamic in Tibetan Buddhism, for instance—but in the West, it is a fact of life, however controversial, and we must look at it, its origins and its history, unflinchingly.

Chapter Two

The Legacy of Monolatry

It is an interesting experience to reread the Old Testament after having spent years immersed in the *via negativa* mysticism of the West. The non-dualistic path of negation that we see in the *Mystical Theology* of Dionysius the Areopagite, or in the sermons of Meister Eckhart, is an entirely different species than what we see in Deuteronomy. To read Deuteronomy is to enter into an alien and alienated world. Yet it is the perspective expressed in Deuteronomy that has been far more influential for the West than any kind of gnostic non-dualism. Hence, before we can delve into questions of gnosis and non-dualism, we have to confront what precedes and in some ways forms the foundation for much of modernity; we have to consider the problems inherent in what I am terming the monotheistic legacy.

I well remember in Sunday School the historical timeline that more than one teacher drew on a blackboard, emphasizing the continuity between the Old and the New Testaments. We assumed, in the tradition of liberal Calvinism, that the god of one was the god of the other, and it never occurred to us that they might not be the same. Such heretical thoughts, expressed by Marcion already in late antiquity, were successfully suppressed then, and did not recur very often since. But all the same, it is jarring to read in Deuteronomy that

> When the Lord your God brings you into the land which you are
> entering to take posession of it, and clears away many nations before you,
> the Hittites, the Girgashites, the Amorites, the Canaanites, the Perizzites,
> the Hivites, and the Jebusites, seven nations greater and mightier than

yourselves, and when the Lord your God gives them over to you, and you defeat them; then you must utterly destroy them; you shall make no covenant with them, and show no mercy to them. You shall not make marriages with them. . . But thus shall you deal with them: you shall break down their altars and dash in pieces their pillars, and hew down their Asherim, and burn their graven images with fire.[23]

Or again, later in the same book, we read again that the Israelites may offer peace to opponents, but their terms of peace are that those who surrender become slaves. Thus for the lands "very far from you," but as to the local tribes, once again, "you shall save alive nothing that breathes, but you shall utterly destroy them," men, women, children, cattle alike.[24]

And the examples can be multipled. Even in Psalms, after the very famous verse "By the waters of Babylon, there we sat down and wept," most people are not aware of the third section enjoining that Babylon must be razed "down to its foundations," and that "Happy shall be he who takes [the Babylonian children] and dashes their brains out against the stones."[25] Or again, when Samuel anoints Saul king of Israel, his first charge is "go and smite Amalek, and utterly destroy all that they have; do not spare them, but kill both man and woman, infant and suckling, ox and sheep, camel and ass."[26] However, Saul did not kill everything that breathed—he kept aside some good animals and the king of the Amalekites he spared—and thus the Lord rejected him as king of Israel.

We need to think here about the significance of these injunctions. One aspect, of course, is the policy of total eradication of the other tribes. Identification with the tribal god of Israel does not allow for peaceful coexistence; the injunctions are absolute. In order to serve this tribal god, one must not only eschew all other gods, but also must in order to possess this land, slaughter men, women, infants, and animals together, leaving alive nothing that breathes. Another aspect is the absolute eradication of the existing religious traditions, which are closely identified with nature. Thus, the Lord enjoins the Israelites not only to slaughter everything that breathes, but also to destroy any sacred stones and to hew down any sacred trees or pillars.

This policy of total eradication of the other—eradication of competing people, and of their religious sites in nature—is effectively a complete evacuation of the land, an utter annihilation not only of surrounding peoples, but also of any trace of them. Even their livestock is to be obliterated, and the Israelites are instructed to show no mercy to anyone nor to make any treaties with tribes whose land they occupy. Thus all preëxisting ancient connections to nature, all signs of ancient sacred sites, or holy trees or pillars are to be struck down and absolutely destroyed. This eradication effectively means that the new people are radically separated from the land's history; nature itself is also alien to them in that all previous human relationships to the land are severed.

Underlying this policy of eradication—which has some interesting parallels to and contrasts with the attitudes of European settlers toward indigenous peoples of the Americas—is a radical anxiety. Regina Schwartz has sagely pointed out that the term "monotheism" is actually inappropriate for describing what we see in the Old Testament, if monotheism is taken to mean that there is only one god.[27] More accurate would be a term like "monolatry," meaning an insistence that people worship a particular god and not others. It is absolutely clear that the tribal god of the Israelites is one deity among a number of tribal deities, and thus he insists that, in the very first of the commandments, he is a jealous deity and will tolerate no other deities before him. Again and again, we read injunctions against following or recognizing other gods—which of course means that there *are* other gods. The Israelites are commanded to destroy so utterly these competing tribes because their deities and their connections to nature pose a kind of existential threat to this particular tribal deity.

But why? This is the great mystery. The underlying dynamic in the Old Testament is implacably dualistic or us/them—but such a dynamic is not the only one possible. A pluralistic ethos of live and let live is at least imaginable. Why the extreme ethos of violent dispossession, of annihilating the other tribes and obliterating all trace of preëxisting sacred landscape? The obliterative drive derives, I am convinced, from the underlying anxiety built into the assertion of one god against a background of other gods, and the anxiety concerning whether wrath would be visited upon the people or tribal favor bestowed by that deity.[28] Built into all of this is the notion of a people who set themselves radically apart from others and from nature—along with a whole series of attendant dualities—and rather than attempting to discern the origins of this dualism, it is more useful here to think about its consequences.

It has become commonplace for ecological writers to see the origin of human separation from nature in Genesis, in the assertion of the creator deity that man shall have dominion over the earth and the creatures of the earth. However, it is simply fact that man has dominion, and not just because it is remarked in Genesis. At the same time, less attention has been paid to the kinds of later injunctions we are considering here, which have the effect of completely sundering one tribe not only from other tribes, but also from the traditional signs of nature religion. It is true that the assertion of human dominion is significant, but more significant is the insistence, later in the Old Testament, on the annihilation of other people who have longstanding religious relationships to the land that are literally fixed by vertical markers: standing stones, pillars, poles, trees.

What matters, then, is strictly *our* human collectivity as against *theirs*. The world that we see in Deuteronomy and in the Old Testament as a whole is one demarcated and indeed governed exclusively by a particular tribal bond to a particular deity, which is elevated to the ambiguous concept of "nation," and at the same time asserted as absolutely superior to all others. This is quite different from the ontological monotheism of Platonism, which is quite accepting of multiple paths to the One, and which accepts nature as good. Monotheism is not necessarily anti-pluralist or anti-nature, in other words. The whole history of Platonism shows that. But the kind of monolatry enjoined in the Old Testament exists precisely because and in the end only because it is anti-pluralist; this is its *raison d'être*.

This brings us to a difficult but central point. The kind of monolatry we see in the Old Testament is inherently exoteric. That is, it is enjoined by outside force, by threat, by the insistence of the tribal god who will punish infidelity to him with terrible curses. The whole operation, in other words, is driven by and overwhelmed with fear. When Tertullian rages against the "pagan" "heretics," he inveighs especially against their rejection of the motivation of fear. This same theme he deploys against Marcion, who argued, with good reason, that the Beatitudes of Jesus represent an ethos motivated not by fear but by love. Tertullian was eager to rejoin that Jesus, too, came to instill fear, as a representative of the same deity we see in the Old Testament.

Here we are touching on the basic architecture built into Judaism, Christianity, and Islam alike, sometimes termed the Abrahamic religions. Christianity and Islam present themselves as, and indeed are, in some respects new revelations. But what is their relationship to this preëxisting tribal deity of the Old Testament, the one who required the slaughter of every man, woman, and child of some competing peoples? To what extent are all three of these traditions inclined toward an inherent dualism built on anxiety and its bigger sibling, fear? To what extent are all three of these religious traditions at a deep level exoteric, that is, built upon a foundation of us/him or us/them dualisms that separate rather than unite peoples, and that divide humanity from nature?

Here I am using the terms *esoteric* and *exoteric* to refer to a dynamic inherent in and perhaps endemic to monotheism or monolatry. This exoteric/esoteric opposition—for that is effectively what it is—derives from the dualistic legacy built into monolatry and enforced through violence that is attributed to the deity via the deity's representatives, but it is fundamentally an opposition between outward assertion and inner concentration. The exoteric approach results in an effort to control others; the esoteric approach represents an inward turn. Those who turn inward are by definition not interested in controlling or judging others; their entire orientation is different.

Exoterism is built into monolatry—the two are inseparable. All of the monolatric traditions assert their own people's convenant with a particular version of the one god, but everything about the covenantal relationship is dualistic; it is effectively an enforced dualism from the very beginning. The god is a jealous god who is quick to inflict punishments or curses upon the covenanted people, let alone upon their competitors; thus, the covenantal relationship itself is fraught with anxiety. It is profoundly divided into I or we/other, and furthermore the fact that the god has to constantly threaten punishment for infidelity has a natural human corollary, which is that the priests or traditional authorities, acting as divine representatives, also must coerce loyalty. Thus the monolatric tradition is inherently exoteric, that is, monolatry is the outward coercion of other people(s) and the ritual placation of the perpetually potentially wrathful tribal deity.

But each of the exoteric monolatrisms nonetheless carry within them some forms of esoterism that make possible the transcendence of this dualistic, antagonistic legacy. Judaism has Kabbalism, Islam has Sufism, and Christianity has more individualistic mysticism. Central to all of these is the *via negativa* mysticism that uses words to point toward what cannot be described and that shatters all conceptualizations of it. In Christianity, we see this first in Basilides, then later in the *Mystical Theology* of Dionysius the Areopagite, and still later in the work of Meister Eckhart and the anonymous author of *The Cloud of Unknowing*. The *via negativa* is not opposed to the exoteric, monolatric tradition in which it exists—rather, it leads straight out of those dualisms.

In all of the covenantal monolatric traditions, mysticism is never central; it cannot be because the primary tradition is exoteric and dualistic. Mysticism, as the transcendence of dualism, is at best tolerated, at worst persecuted by the mainstream exoteric tradition to which it is always ancillary. Mysticism is esoteric—it is pure esoterism, in that it is the individual experience of inner awakening that cannot be conveyed to anyone else, only alluded to. Here, of course, we're referring to what we might call pure or archetypal mysticism of the Basilidean or Dionysian line, and not to visionary mysticism, though similar observations may hold in those cases too. The central problem here is the tension between exoteric and esoteric, endemic to the three monolatries of Judaism, Christianity, and Islam.

The term "exoteric" usually refers to the outward or public forms of a religious tradition, but actually, I think there is a particular and extreme exoteric-esoteric tension endemic to the Abrahamic monotheisms. This tension comes from the presence, in the Abrahamic monotheisms, of what we may term an extreme exoterism present in all three primary traditions. By extreme exoterism, I mean the intense dualism that is built into monolatry, and that insists on defining itself by excluding, indeed, anathematizing others. Extreme exoterism generates—it is the engine of—the religious fanaticism characteristic of modern fundamentalism.

Extreme exoterism insists upon the forcible assertion of a particular monolatry and its associated traditions upon people designated as radically other. Extreme exoterism is visible in all three monotheisms. We see its ur-expression in the Old Testament, in particular in texts like Deuteronomy, which present the archetypal form of what we see repeated in numerous subsequent venues, wherever people claiming a special covenantal relationship with God take over a land and subjugate or expel its inhabitants. But we also see extreme exoterism at work in the construction of the Inquisitional apparatus in Catholicism, and indeed, wherever an Inquisitor feels/is invested with an obligation to enforce official theology or ideology upon the population "for their own good." And we see extreme exoterism at work in Islam, in the fanatical belief that all peoples should be subjugated, forced to submit to exoteric Islam.

Extreme exoterism is behavior motivated by fear. Fear, of course, is radically dualistic—one is afraid of the radically other, the hostile or potentially hostile opponent. Interestingly, this is the relationship inherent in covenantal monolatry—over and over, we read in the Old Testament that God is become wrathful, that he will abandon his people, that he has abandoned them, that he will curse and punish them, and so forth. This same relationship is extended outward toward those whose land one wishes to appropriate, and toward those whom one designates as "heretics" or as in some other way radically other. Such a relationship is also visible in modern Muslim jihadism against non-Muslim modernity. Why did the Roman Catholic Church persecute the Cathars, who themselves were pacifist? Fear that they represented an ideological/theological threat, and a belief that by subjugating and annihilating them, one was doing God's work.

Esoterism, on the other hand, at heart is desire for union. This underlying motivation is why, when we survey the history of Western esotericism, what we find is that while esoterists are themselves frequently persecuted, they do not persecute others.[29] This is a consistent pattern, visible all the way back to late antiquity at least. The esoterist is interested in a richer inner life, in changes in consciousness that bring one closer to knowledge of and union with the divine, with humanity, and with nature. Such a union is, of course, exactly the reverse of what we see in exoterism, which consists in the objectification and subjugation of the other. Here, again, exoteric and esoteric primarily refer to mental tendencies or inclinations, the purest forms of which are visible in, on the one hand, the Inquisitor, on the other, the *via negativa* mystic.

While it is true that exoterism is built into monolatry, exoterism as the term is used here refers to a basic human tendency that is not tied to or found only in monolatric religious traditions. One sees the same exoteric dynamic operating in twentieth-century totalitarian states, including China and North Korea. Here, exoterism refers to the tendency captured so tellingly in Dostoevsky's character of the Grand Inquisitor, who saw himself as a divine instrument to control others for their own and for society's good. The attempt to bring about an earthly paradise through force inevitably produces a nightmare, be it Stalin's gulags, Pol Pot's killing fields, or Mao's cultural revolution.

But where are the communities created around esoteric inspiration rather than exoteric compulsion? This is an interesting question. Examples of exoteric communities are numerous, whereas instances of esoteric communities are rather few, to put it mildly. Those who seek to institute an Islamic caliphate, what is their dream? Is it not redolent of the Taliban's closed, punitive theocracy? Or again, those who imagine an American theocracy, of what do they dream, if not to impose their exoteric vision upon their fellow citizens "for their own good"? Such dystopias have no room for Sufi or for Christian mystics; indeed, the mystics seem threatening to the dystopians.

Understanding the nature of exoterism is extremely important because there are other ways of organizing communities, but it is in the nature of exoterism to totally occlude and anathematize all alternatives.

By now the outlines of our investigation ought to be fairly clear: in order to explore the possibility of new cultures, we will need to pursue what could be termed, after Gershom Scholem, a "counter-history," or after Michel Foucault, an expedition of intellectual archaeology. It is vital that we examine a bit more just what happened in late antiquity at the point when Christian "orthodoxy" and "heresies" emerged, for it is here that we see on the one hand the dualistic basis of "orthodoxy," and on the other, the non-dualistic basis of the Basilidean gnosis, for this division will have far-reaching consequences. In short, it is high time for us to explore further the counter-history of the West in relation to what is often termed "postmodernity."

Chapter Three

Counter-History and the "Postmodern Dilemma"

In the late twentieth and early twenty-first centuries, the term "postmodern" entered common usage as a reference to what many intellectuals posited would follow the modern period, whatever that is. Of course, this neologism never made much sense etymologically, since "modern" by definition refers to the present, and "postmodern" thus could only mean "post-now." But "postmodernism" was not merely a species of post-nowish futurism—the term also was freighted with an array of implications concerning "meta-narratives" and "essentialism." Postmodernism was widely taken to refer to a culturally fragmented world in which "meta-narratives" and belief in "essences" are seen as suspect, and in which cultures and identities are seen to be mere social constructions or projections. As such, postmodernism does not provide a vantage point for social or cultural action, because it cannot: it derives from the absence or rejection of such vantage points, and in this is its fundamental dilemma. Its adherents can describe; they even can create marvelous labyrinthine intellectual constructs; yet there can be no postmodern socio-political movement, for by definition, adherents must withhold affirmation. But in so doing, as we shall see, they paradoxically create an opening for negative theology, that is, for gnosis.

Whence came postmodernism? Postmodernism came about as a secular response to the brutalities of totalitarianism, to the realization that modernity had given birth, not to utopia but dystopia, not only to dreams but also to nightmares and millions of corpses. After World War

II, the Frankfurt school sought to understand how it was that Nazism emerged in Germany, and how totalitarianism could take root in a "developed" Western industrial nation; but it was not until the last quarter of the twentieth century that postmodernism appeared, right around the time that the Soviet Union collapsed. Dissidents, including Solzhenitsyn, had made clear much earlier that Communism had provided no earthly paradise, any more than did its siblings Fascism and National Socialism. The fall of the Soviet Union actually occurred for much of the Left with the slow realization that Communism actually had meant dictatorship, mass murder, and brutal gulags. Postmodernism—as the rejection of grand meta-narratives that ultimately result in death camps—is in many respects a healthy reaction to the monstrous history of the twentieth century, to the enticing fictions of a workers' paradise or of a secular millennium. From this perspective, postmodernism is a refusal to be fooled again.

But postmodernism also entails socio-political stasis. It reflects, but it can provide no basis for action. We see this very clearly in the work of Jean Baudrillard (1929-2007), for example. Baudrillard's work, he complained, is frequently said to be "brilliant," but rarely regarded as "serious." Why? Baudrillard is an analyst of fragmented modern industrial society and in particular of media: he reflects, again and again, on the "virtual reality" of modern media-saturated society, and as a series of reflections, Baudrillard's work is like a carnival house of mirrors. His focus is on the image, and "the image is bound neither to truth nor to reality; it is appearance and bound to appearance."[30] Because his perpetual concern is the image-saturated house of illusions that is media-driven modern society, his wry reflections on this society never stray beyond it because they cannot. He remarks, for instance, that people today might well "rather be dominated by machines," perhaps we even "prefer an impersonal, automatic domination" that "absolves us of any personal responsibility." Machines, he continues, are entirely irresponsible, and we are coming to resemble them.[31] But he can offer only wry critique.

In effect, Baudrillard's work represents an "end of history" not by transcendence or apocalypse, but by impasse. Baudrillard himself writes that the postmodern era represents "the end of revolutions (and of history in general)." It is, he thinks, "no longer a question of history in progress, of a directive schema, or of regulation by crisis," because "the logic of history" has been "obliterated by the dizzying whirl of change."[32] There remains only an antagonism between "global power and terrorism," between "virtual omnipotence and those fiercely opposed to it."

Baudrillard's work, like that of many who are styled "postmodern-ist," reveals a secular dead end, a self-reflecting hall of mirrors in which, wherever humanity looks, it sees only its own virtual selves and virtual illusions. It is a world of abstract words and of shining commercial im-ages, and it is also a world in which the dirt and the wind, the trees and animals and nitty-gritty of life appear not to exist. Of course, all these things, just like history, do continue to exist outside the hall of media mirrors, but the "postmodern" worldview—which derives from Marshall McLuhan's notion of a media-saturated and media-determined society, and perhaps from the Teilhardian notion of a "noösphere"—simply ig-nores those things. Adherents of such a worldview see only abstractions, whose nebulous opacity obscures for them the rough-hewn timbers, the stones and the clouds of the actual world.

Such a blindness is perhaps not too far from the world-blindness of the architects of Communist or National Socialist nightmares, for whom actual people and the physical world were also obscured by lofty abstrac-tions of "national goals" or "the good of the people," or the "ideals of the Cultural Revolution," or whatnot. But someone like Baudrillard clearly is not interested in translating his ironic observations about media or virtual reality into any kind of political, social, or cultural agenda. Indeed, it is as though his whole work emerges out of a refusal or an incapacity for action—his chosen role is as the ironic observer, as annotator of a world of illusory images.

Thus the work of Baudrillard, and indeed, much of the phenom-enon grouped under the heading of "postmodernism," could be read as an opportunity, as a particular historic moment when intellectuals on the political Left had abandoned the metanarratives that had led to the totalitarianisms of the twentieth century, and when it was theoretically possible to move in an entirely new direction. But where? This is what I refer to as the "postmodern dilemma." The Left has nowhere to turn, no possible new direction, if it has indeed abandoned any ideas of univer-sals or essences, metanarratives or metaphysics. Without these, without some metaphysical ground upon which to stand, "postmoderns" are lost in a fog or in a house of self-reflecting mirrors. This is the impasse that Baudrillard represents as well as anyone. What to do?

One could begin with history or, to be more accurate, with counter-history. If one did, the perspective of Gershom Scholem would be par-ticularly valuable. Scholem, the pioneering historian of esoteric Judaism, held that the way beyond the impasse presented by rationalist positivism lay first of all in a reëxamination of history. When one has reached an impasse, it is necessary to return to history and understand what went wrong, what paths had been ignored or suppressed, and hence what alternative avenues were. This process has been termed the writing of "counter-history," and in Scholem's case, it consisted in inverting the rationalism of his academic predecessors so as to see if "what was termed degeneracy will be thought of as a revelation and light," "a great living myth," "the discovery of hidden life by removal of the obfuscating masks."[33] We are called, Scholem tells us, to find the courage to "penetrate through the symbolic plain and through the wall of history."[34] Of course, if we liked, we could replace the term "counter-history" with "esoteric history."

But in any case, it is important to explore further the central concept here. If we are to understand more clearly how we have come to a present impasse, we must retrace the steps that led us to it, and ideally, we must return to the very first point at which we set out on that particular path. Only when we are, metaphorically speaking, at this original fork do we have the possibility of taking a different path. Of course, such a reconsideration of history is not merely for the sake of accumulating new information, however valuable that is—rather, counter-history potentially offers the recovery of what has been lost or ignored. By careful investigation, it is possible to reässemble and even reïntegrate what had formerly been rejected, and thus find a way beyond the impasse.

Here is a possible application of this idea. Conventional narratives of Western history usually run upon rails laid already in late antiquity on the arguments advanced by heresiophobes like Irenaeus and Tertullian, who vilified the very idea of gnosis, that is to say, of direct spiritual knowledge that includes and transcends ratiocinative knowledge. Heresiophobia, or anti-gnosis, was fixed in place by a series of Church Councils that emphasized church dogmas centering on belief or doctrinal acquiescence. What became "orthodox" Christianity did so primarily not as an affirmation, but as a denial or refusal, a turning away from what we see, for instance, in the work of Basilides and his school in the second century. The rejection of gnosis, of the very idea of gnosis, is a theme traceable from late antiquity forward through the medieval period and right up into the modern era. Indeed, one could even make the case that (to turn Hans Blumenberg's hypothesis on its head) the "Enlightenment" was in fact a renewed rejection of gnosis in favor of rationalism, and that this second rejection of gnosis (with a corresponding affirmation of rationalist dualism) is what created modernity.

We sketch here the outlines of a master narrative (the rejection

36

of gnosis) that leads in one direction, but also of a possible counter-narrative or counter-history that leads in a very different direction. An author whose middle work at times implied the possibility of this kind of counter-history is Peter Sloterdijk (1947-). His books, beginning with *Critique of Cynical Reason* (1983), tangentially recognize what I have termed the "postmodern dilemma," and so sometimes point toward Asian religious traditions, in particular Taoism, as well as toward Jewish and Christian mysticism or even Gnosticism as possible avenues to its resolution.[35] Sloterdijk does not undertake any kind of counter-history along the lines I am suggesting, but some of his remarks, particular in his earlier works, could be taken to imply such a possible inquiry, even if as a "postmodernist" he could not commit himself to what might be revealed in such an inquiry.

But at the same time, we have to consider the distinction between counter-history and the reïntegration of what might be discovered through a counter-historical exploration. It is one thing to undertake a counter-historical investigation, and another to determine what to do about it. Is it possible for a counter-historical exploration to provide anything substantial for us existentially? Suppose we do intellectually recover something of Basilides' teachings from late antiquity. Then what? Here we encounter the hidden assumptions of our own time that prevent us from seeing how or even that there are other metaphysical possibilities than those that we take for granted. Once we trace our way back to a fateful historical juncture, once we find the vital node at which counter-history and conventional history meet, we then have a choice. One possibility is to remain fairly strictly as an historical investigator and for the most part leave it at that. This was the choice of Gershom Scholem, the great scholar of Kabbalah, who was not, after all, himself a Kabbalist. Another possibility is to seek to understand for oneself what one has discovered, and this is the choice advocated by Scholem's longtime correspondent, Martin Buber (1878-1965).

Buber argued that while reason and sensory experience (*Erfahrung*) are important, there is another kind of experience—ecstatic spiritual experience (*Erlebnis*)—that transcends linguistic expression. This ecstatic spiritual experience is direct spiritual perception, or gnosis, and in discussing it, Buber drew from the writings of Meister Eckhart, as well as from Nicholas of Cusa and Jacob Böhme, on whom he had done his doctoral work. Although the gnostic inevitably seeks to express this inexpressible experience, in fact it cannot be conveyed through language except indirectly. This indirect expression is the origin of mythology—the history of religion is thus the chronicle of progressive ossification of original primary insight or gnosis, which must again be individually rediscovered.

Scholem opposed Buber's theory of gnosis, partly for strategic reasons (in order to make space for his own historico-religious investigations), partly as a reflection of his own proclivities toward history and toward language, and partly because linguistic mysticism (language as a means of esoteric transmission) is so deeply imbedded in Jewish Kabbalah throughout its history. Buber's viewpoint, seen from the historian's perspective, seems to reject both history and Kabbalistic tradition in favor of a timeless present that, in the end, cannot be made the object of academic study at all. Thus it would appear that the two positions are irreconcilable.

But the positions are reconcilable once one realizes that they refer to two different realms that are ultimately more complementary than oppositional. Scholem, as the historian of religion, necessarily recognizes that in history and, to go one step deeper, in language itself are embedded clues about the hidden dimensions of existence. Buber recognized something similar, which is why he compiled the personal accounts of mystics into books. But Buber also sought to penetrate beyond historical accounts, beyond intellectual investigation, and reveal different, direct individual experiences (*Erlebnis*) of timelessness. These approaches are complementary because the first emphasizes how time (history and language) can convey hints of timelessness, whereas the second emphasizes how timelessness can be glimpsed in time.

These two complementary perspectives are in fact visible in the seminal work of theosopher Gottfried Arnold (1666-1714), entitled *Unparteiische Kirchen-und-Ketzerhistorie [Impartial Church and Heretic History]* (1699-1700). Arnold's history of the Christian Church is vitally important because, for the first time, an historian of Christianity had set forth a clear typology that distinguished between inner and outer or esoteric and exoteric Christianity. Inner Christianity is authentic Christianity: its adherents are concerned with their own spiritual and moral development. Authentic Christianity is not a secular or worldly institution, nor is it even concerned with worldly institutions or power—its history is solely the record of practitioners of like mind. Outer Christianity, on the other hand, is in fact secular: its adherents are primarily concerned with controlling *other people's* behavior. Secular Christianity seeks to coerce people, to impose dogmatic formulations on them, and even goes so far as to persecute those who belong to inner, authentic Christianity. Conventional Christian history in fact chronicles secular Christianity, its dogmatic formulators, its potentates, and its periodic inquisitional fevers.

But authentic, living Christianity does not belong to the history of secular Christianity—rather, it represents an illumination, a cutting-through of history by timeless direct spiritual experience or gnosis. Whereas in many other religious traditions, religious illumination invigorates or reinvigorates religious institutions, in Christian history all too often the religious institutions or their representatives respond by attempting to silence or kill gnostics as "heretics." But of course, as Arnold points out, historically persecution is one of the distinguishing signs of authentic Christianity, beginning with the Crucifixion of Christ himself. Thus the secular Church in effect represents the same worldly spirit (*spiritus mundi*) that imperial Rome did, and is all too often bitterly opposed to those who seek timeless illumination or gnosis.

Why the emphasis on Christian origins? As Weber and many others recognized, secular modernity emerged first in Christendom, and if we are to find an alternative path to the one that led to the rationalism and technicism of modernity, we must search back to that point at which we first see a major fork in the road. That initial and primary fork in the road is not to be found in Protestantism, nor in medieval Christianity—it is much earlier. We find the primary confluence of alternative paths in late antiquity, during the period when Christianity could have gone in the gnostic direction indicated by Basilides, or in the anti-gnostic direction indicated by Tertullian, who went so far as to speculate that the persecution of "heretics" might even continue posthumously! Only in Christianity do we find such a deep polarization between the "orthodox" and the gnostic "heretics." This division, so fundamental to Christianity's history, has a deep connection to the emergence of secular modernity—a connection that we will explore shortly.

Gottfried Arnold was right. There is much to be learned by looking anew at the history of Christianity, setting aside the accumulated interpretive baggage of past millennia, and focusing instead on essential signposts or *kennzeichen* (literally: 'signs for knowing') in order to understand history in a new way. When we do this, we begin to see not only history, but also our own contemporary world in a different light. Is it possible to find in Gnosticism something like a 'red thread' that could lead us out of the labyrinth and back into daylight and the real world? That is the possibility suggested by Arnold's massive reinterpretation of Christianity.

Thus when we return to what I have termed the "postmodern di-lemma," we begin to see not just a dead-end road, but also perhaps an opportunity to fundamentally reconsider what brought us to this current point. Having reached a kind of *cul-de-sac,* we are compelled by that fact alone to reflect upon how we came there, and on what new path we might embark. One of the essential problems of modernity—arguably even *the* essential problem of modernity—is that proposals for social reform, for new intellectual constructs, for solutions to the dilemmas that confront us, almost invariably derive from within modernity itself. As a result, what initially sounds attractive—the social redistributionism of Marx, for example—soon reveals itself to be monstrous in the application. The "postmodern dilemma" is at core a realization of this problem, to which, however, the "postmodern" theorist can offer no resolution. The resolution has to come from outside modernity itself, from *beyond.* In order to understand this point more clearly, we must begin with the age-old subject that can never be fully vanquished: nature.

Chapter Four

Nature

The fundamental problems of modernity are its omnivorousness and its self-enclosure. These are, of course, the two sides of one coin. On the one side is the relentless appetite of consumerist humanity to consume everything it possibly can, an appetite that (on the other side) assumes only the human world counts. Consumerist society requires the constant conversion of the natural world into abstraction, that is, into capital, commodity, consumed object. What is gained by this conversion? An ever-more-complex human realm, a human society that exists more and more in a virtual human world separated from its own historical or traditional roots and from the natural world that it rapaciously uses up. But this trajectory away from the earth, away from nature, cannot continue indefinitely.

What I have termed the "postmodern dilemma" in fact exemplifies a trajectory away from the natural world into abstraction and into the virtual, that is, into a realm of representation. But "postmodernism" is far from alone in this trajectory—rather, postmodern discourse is symptomatic of a much broader and deeper social trajectory away from nature and away from human conviviality. We see this tendency exemplified not only in the phenomenon of consumerism, but also in its attendants, social fragmentation and the decline of the extended family, the disappearance of small town and rural life, the disappearance of traditional religion, and the emergence of religious and political fundamentalisms. All of these tendencies help to create a world characterized by extreme individualism, ultimately, by a kind of solipsism.

We see this solipsist tendency also in the broad emphasis on social constructivism during the late twentieth and early twenty-first centuries. If "metanarratives" and "essences" are to be regarded as taboo, then what is left? How did the human world come into being? All aspects of society, which is effectively "the world," are thus conceived as constructed, not revealed or given—amusingly, even mysticism [!] came to be so construed.[36] In all these tendencies, intellectual and social alike, we see an overarching emphasis on the human social world as self-enclosed, self-created, and all-encompassing. Such a perspective is intensified in a world defined by mass media, by images and worlds, by "events" that are virtually inseparable from entertainment. Humanity might then be seen as trapped in a hall of mirrors, in a kind of carnivalesque spectacle of the perpetually reflected self. What is beyond the human self? Or is everything, "everything," a human construct?

Western Political Paralysis

At the same time that we saw the emergence of a totally anthropocentric world, we saw the almost total inability of liberal parliamentary governments to confront the destruction of the natural world or, for that matter, nearly any of the great problems confronting humanity. Parliamentary or representative governments, and particularly that of the United States, seemed as incapable of solving problems in the early twenty-first century as their Weimar counterparts in the early twentieth century—rather than making decisions with an eye toward the benefit of future generations, nearly all decisions were made in order to achieve short-term, expedient, or mercenary goals.

On reflection, we can see that this political paralysis has its origins in the same tendencies that we saw in "postmodernism"—that is, in an absence of metaphysical or even cosmological moorings. If "everything" is merely a construct, if there is nothing essential or transcendent, if all metanarratives are to be distrusted, then what is left but the narrative of the self and what is good for it? Narcissism, short-term personal or immediate gain becomes the primary criterion for decision-making, and why not, if we are indeed living in a hall of reflective mirrors?

Of course, some claimed that the American Republican party hegemony of the early twenty-first century, based to some considerable degree upon evangelical and fundamentalist Christianity, represented a return to metaphysical and cosmological moorings, but did it? As the historian John Lukacs, as well as numerous traditional conservatives pointed out during that period, "conservatism" of the Republican variety in fact represented a repudiation of virtually all traditionally conservative principles in favor of expediency and power.[37] The truth is, one can hardly find a single Republican initiative during the entire period of the hegemony that could be termed traditionally conservative. This was an era of widespread legislative corruption combined with military adventurism and extreme fiscal irresponsibility—to which Republicans added fealty to radical globalism and the consequent policies of de-industrialization and de-agrification of the United States.

What about the notion that evangelical Protestantism represented a return to metaphysical moorings? In some respects, this is arguably true, particularly where evangelicalism and fundamentalism intersect. A fundamentalist emphasis on the literal historical truth of Scripture does represent a kind of socio-religious anchor, an historical metanarrative that in turn offers clear and simple answers to many prevailing social issues. However, such an historical metanarrative (that begins with a literal interpretation of Genesis, and concludes with an historical apocalypse) does not truly offer metaphysical moorings—what it offers, rather, is an historical narrative with some apparent socio-political implications.

What we see, in both these political and religious spheres, is an almost absolute emphasis on human society. Evangelicalism, especially of the fundamentalist variety, is focused on a narrative of human history, and its theologians and adherents have no interest in negative theology or in nature—what matters is historical faith, adherence to a set of theological doctrines, and assertion of particular socio-political stances like opposition to abortion. Likewise, to the extent that one can discern any coherent ideology, Republicanism represents adherence to a set of political doctrines, among them a quasi-religious faith in globalist trade for multi-national corporations, and in those expedient socio-political stances that ensure continued support of some evangelical Christians. Both Evangelicalism and Republicanism turn on an historical narrative that leads toward an "end of history," that is, toward a quasi-millennial or millennialist state for humanity, in which nature has little or no role. Both ideologies assume the absolute centrality of humanity and the peripherality or near non-existence of nature.

Thus it is perhaps not surprising that one also finds in both groups a widespread dislike, if not outright hatred, of environmentalists. One can understand this antipathy better when one recognizes that environmentalists or ecologists speak, at least to some extent, on behalf of nature—that is, on behalf of what is outside the realm of artificial human constructs. Neither evangelical Protestantism nor Republicanism are in the least interested in what exists outside the realm of human society and its laws. In their view, nature exists to be used, to be consumed, to serve as raw materials for industrial society, or to be "left behind" after the "rapture." Those who speak on behalf of nature thus offer a disturbing counter-narrative of human destructiveness, of historical decline rather than progress.

Of course, environmentalists or ecologists (even those of the "deep ecology" strain) make no profound metaphysical claims, and in fact environmentalism also derives from an historical narrative, of which "deep ecology" is the most extreme form. In this narrative, humanity can look ahead toward an environmental apocalypse, or toward a millennialist state in which nature is preserved, but in either case, it is a matter of an historical dialectic between human society and nature. To privilege wilderness over urban human civilization represents a critique of anthropocentrism, to be sure, but the dialectic remains "horizontal," that is, between human society and "the environment." The sacred, the "vertical" does not intrude into this new narrative, whose most extreme form is the exact negation or inversion of the mainstream Republican narrative that privileges human society over nature.

So long as it remains on a "horizontal" level as an historical narrative of the dialectic between society and its environment, environmentalism can offer no compelling or overarching perspective. Instead, it is the convenient opponent of consumerism or corporationism, offering its contribution to a secular version of the dualistic opposition between God and Satan, the One and the Anti-One, the Yes and the No. But which is "yes," and which "no"? This depends upon which narrative one accepts: the narrative of progress, or the narrative of decline—for God and the Devil switch roles depending upon which is one's master narrative. But either way, it is a narrative of dualities, of opposition—and it remains inevitably temporal, linear, horizontal.

Modern political paralysis has its origins in such binary oppositions, which remain always limited to a secular horizon. The totalitarian nightmares of communism and fascism, deriving as they did from secular millennialist visions of the future, were primarily concerned with the transformation of human society, with creating a "new man" or a " new humanity" and a "new world." These ideologies rested upon a dualistic foundation, and having seen their consequences, it is not surprising that subsequent liberal parliamentary societies would be more inclined to paralysis than to run the risk of again creating totalitarian nightmares. But we must recognize that all of these modern political models assume a strict historicism, a this-worldliness, and as a result, are perpetually inclined toward dreaming of another secular millennium.

In fact, the fundamental political structure in modernity is national socialism. As Italian scholarship has demonstrated, Italian fascism represented a "heresy of the left," that is, it represents a branch from communism. But what characterizes communism and fascism as political constructs, if not the deep union of corporations and government? In the case of Communist China, one sees state ownership and control of companies, whereas in the United States, for example, one sees something closer to corporate ownership and control (via lobbying and other mechanisms) of the government via ownership and control of politicians. In either case, the military-corporate bureaucracies remain the porous center that unites corporations and government.

Practically speaking, there are only fairly limited distinctions between modern industrial forms of governmental/political structures. Communist China, Post-Soviet Russia, the United States, the European Union, Japan, and so forth—all featured strong centralized governmental bureaucracies, covert or overt military-industrial-corporate complexes, and oligopolic corporations tied in closely to the national government via political "donations," "lobbying," or plain bribery. The process of corporate globalization in the late twentieth and early twenty-first centuries resulted in fundamental similarities in national bureaucratic and political structures, regardless of whether the nation-state was putatively "liberal" or "communist" or "authoritarian." What one sees is ever-greater centralized power accruing to transnational corporations and to central or federal governments.

Yet at the same time, one sees no clear example of any of these centralized political structures valuing nature for its own sake. Furthermore, given the global economic system that had emerged by the early twenty-first century, one can scarcely imagine how such alternative values might appear within a closed-loop system based upon socio-economic valuation, that is, upon exploitation and consumption. The bizarre nature of modern socio-economics becomes clearer when we realize that destruction (through war, catastrophe, terrorism, whatever) is economically privileged (because it is "activity") over preservation (because preservation by definition is *not* "activity"). According to this widely accepted modern economic model, the obliteration of a city "boosts" the city's "economy" because of all the subsequent necessary rebuilding. Economic "activity," consumption of everything as quickly as possible, is thus privileged over preservation or conservation. There is, in the modern global political order, little incentive for conservation of anything, let alone conservation of nature.

Given this global economic background, one is hardly surprised to discover widespread political paralysis not only in the United States, but indeed globally. There are very few examples of nations whose leaders have decided to privilege the preservation of traditional cultures and of nature over exploitation and consumption. An exception is the nation of Bhutan, whose Buddhist aristocracy decided that they would seek to preserve their traditional culture and the natural beauty of their country-side, accepting some aspects of modernity, but only on their own terms. But globally, such a case is more than unusual. As a result, the natural world is under siege almost everywhere—in the oceans, in the air, in the mountains, in the forests, on the remaining glaciers . . .

The truth is that in the global economic-political order, nature does not exist.

Towards a Metaphysics of Nature

This brings us to fundamental questions concerning nature. We already have observed how modernity has tended more and more toward Babel—that is, toward humanity building a tower of its own devising, separated more and more from earth and from nature. "Postmodern theory" for the most part reflects this same tendency toward the abstract, and toward a world of ever-more-complex human rationalizations, of ever-greater cleverness that is also evermore separated from the natural world, from gritty sand and wind, from black loam and growing green seedlings. "Critical theory" is only a mirror reflection of global capitalism in its reductio ad nihilum of nature.

The widespread assumption, in modernity, is that nature has no metaphysical status, because, of course, nothing has any metaphysical status any more. We are, according to this view, as Baudrillard would have it, left in the "desert of the Real." But of course, the "real," in this case, is precisely the "unreal," that is, it is the desert of the merely virtual, the realm of human-created images. And indeed, if we accept this perspective, then nature could be said to exist only in relation to the human world that converts it into images or simulacra. Even if we don't accept this line of analysis, still, in the global corporationist order, nature does not exist except as "resources," as "raw materials," that is, as grist for the industrial mills. Here too, nature has no metaphysical status.

And indeed, how could it? After all, whether or not we accept the Weberian view that global corporationism emerged from Protestantism or more broadly, from historicist Christianity, the fact remains that in historicist Christianity, nature's metaphysical status was always notoriously uncertain. It's true that, after the ecological awakening that began in the 1960s and 1970s, there emerged Christian apologists who sought to find in Francis of Assisi, for instance, a peg on which to hang a Christian environmentalism. But such efforts always seemed contrived or forced, whereas it seemed only natural when Christian apocalypticism was married to global corporationism under the banner of the Republican party beginning in the Reagan era, encapsulated in the well-known remark of Reagan's Interior Secretary James Watt that we humans might as well use up nature now, because the apocalyptic return of Christ is just around the corner. However crude, such a remark does perfectly sum up the union of global capitalism and historicist Christianity, within which nature has no metaphysical status.

Given our contemporary ambience, is there any basis upon which we could establish a metaphysics today? Or are we indeed, as so many would claim, adrift or lost in space, with no real anchors or reference points? To answer such questions, let us go back to Greek philosophy, and in particular to the Platonic tradition. Plato, we will recall, in *Republic*, proposed the allegory of the Cave, and the idea that what we see in this world is akin to a shadow-play cast upon a wall. Nature, such an analogy suggests, thus is but a reflection of a greater reality, sometimes termed the realm of Ideas. Plotinus continued this line of thought in the third of his *Enneads*, and it is here that we begin to see the basis from which to understand the metaphysical status of nature.

In a signally important passage, Plotinus described exactly how one comes to understand metaphysics—not through ratiocination, but through direct contemplative knowledge, or gnosis. Plotinus writes

From this basis we proceed:
In the advancing stages of Contemplation rising from that in Nature, to that in the Soul, and thence again to that in the Intellectual Principle itself—the object contemplated becomes progressively a more and more intimate possession of the Contemplating Beings, more and more one

thing with them; and in the advanced Soul the objects of knowledge, well on the way towards the Intellectual Principle, are close to identity [with the Contemplator].

Hence we may conclude that, in the Intellectual Principle Itself, there is complete identity of Knower and Known.[38]

Here we see a metaphysics based not on ratiocination or external comparison, but upon inner and direct, non-dualistic understanding. This is the key. What we see in modernity is the end-state or result of a long-standing tradition of what we may term "externalism," or to put it another way, of emphasizing action and outward, manipulative or technical cleverness over inward comprehension of the kind represented here by Plotinus.

Allow me to put it another way. If we privilege manipulative cleverness and ratiocination, then to that extent has nature no metaphysical status because nature is reduced to a collection of objects or resources to be manipulated or consumed. But if we turn to inward contemplative knowledge or gnosis, then nature *does* have metaphysical status, which is comprehensible by an entirely different kind of awareness than what I am terming manipulative cleverness. The metaphysical status of nature, in other words, is only revealed through an "inward bent," that is through the orientation of the mind upon itself or upon its own transcendent origin.[39] The metaphysical status of nature is not, in itself, central but rather is a byproduct of an entire change in the orientation of the mind from the dualism of an objectified world and instead toward an inward unity of subject and object.

What I have termed the "postmodern dilemma" is thus symptomatic of a kind of externalist mentality or orientation characteristic of modernity as a whole, and that inexorably results in what we could call the "anthropization" of the world, that is, the absorption of all of nature into the sphere of human manipulation. The dilemma is that there is seemingly no way out of this anthropization of the world; and there is seemingly no avenue to metaphysics from such a world. This is why modern philosophy finds itself in a *cul-de-sac*. There is nowhere for it to go, except if, as Nicholas Berdyaev did, a philosopher were to return to the experiential metaphysics that we see in the work of Plotinus.

In other words, the metaphysical status of nature could be seen as a kind of sign, an indicator of the turn toward the contemplative path. For after all, what could reveal the metaphysical status of nature except the inner contemplative ascent toward the unity of the knower and the known? Once this is given voice or words, it becomes obvious. There is no external way out of the modern dilemma; there is no external way to "restore" myth or to "return" to a metaphysics of nature—there is only the possibility of a turn inward or what we may term the experiential path of contemplative ascent.

And what is the sign that we have begun to discern a metaphysics of nature? It is that we begin to *leave nature alone.* Is this not what is meant by sacred groves, sacred mountains, sacred rivers? These are places of vision, places where we may attain inner vision, that is, places conducive to contemplation, to the realization of That of which nature itself is a reflection. It is telling that modernity could be characterized as a perspective in which no place is sacred, or to put it another way, as profanation. Another way to put it is this: modernity is effectively the absence of metaphysics, the horizontalization and profanation of the world; and we can recognize the existence of metaphysics by the correlative sign of recognizing sacredness in nature.

The apparent barrenness or vacuity of modernity results from the lack of inward vision, without which the people perish. What I am suggesting is that the destructive dimensions of modernity, right along with its greatest achievements, derive, ultimately, from an orientation of the mind outward toward what we could call technical, ratiocinative, or manipulative consciousness, or cleverness. But cleverness is not the same as wisdom. And it is no accident that, as modern technical and economic apparatus has gained more and more sophistication and power, as society has grown more bureaucratic and complex, one finds in the West fewer and fewer who are devoted to the inward or contemplative life. We will not think our way past the ecological destruction we have wrought; we will not think our way to a new metaphysics of nature. Required, rather, is contemplative vision.

But we should not let the word "vision" deceive us too much. One might be inclined to emphasize that "I" see a particular wild vista, that is, to rest on the comfortable division between subject and object and the idea that "I" am seeing "it." However, the word "vision" here refers not just to outward sight, but also to inward comprehension. To "see" is to identify with, to comprehend, and ultimately, to recognize inner union with that which is seen. When we see that deep mountain valley under the open blue sky, we also are recognizing what that valley and sky are manifestations of—if we may so put it. There is in us a recognition that is also a comprehension, a union of seer with what is seen—and through them both, with what is not seen. "Vision," in other words, includes the transcendence of vision.

What I am suggesting here is not perennialism or universalism, that is, an artificial rational construct of a perennial philosophy or a universal religion projected to be at the center of all religions. Universalism or perennialism is a modern construct—it is the reversed reflection of modern fragmentation, projecting in its place a universal unity. I don't embrace or attack these modern concepts. Rather, I am suggesting something quite different, something that is visible in the work of Basilides and Plotinus in late antiquity, but that by the modern era had almost completely vanished. I am suggesting that what is missing from modern industrialism or rationalism is an experiential union of the individual not only with nature, but also with what transcends nature.

This, after all, is arguably what "metaphysics" means—the individual transcendence of physics, the revelation of what is beyond or "above" nature. That which is beyond or "above" nature is verifiable—through direct experience of it. That direct experience is gnosis. Plotinus refers to this direct experience as contemplation or as contemplative ascent toward realization of the unity of the Knower and of the Known. Basilides refers to this experience in negative terms, as an awareness of *ouk on theos*, or "Not-being God," as the transcendence of that which is perceived by the senses or conceived by ratiocination. Of course there are many others in Western tradition who have also emphasized the importance of direct experiential realization of metaphysical or transcendent reality beyond "nature." But the essential point remains the same: here, gnosis is not an intellectual system or construct—it is, rather, experienced directly by the individual through contemplation.

Seen from this perspective, "postmodernism" is no different than modernism, that is to say, than any other worldview based on ratiocentrism and the corresponding objectification of the world. "Postmodern theory" is simply an intellectually sophisticated form of modernism more generally, and this is why it does not lead to any alternatives, but rather remains inextricably fastened to contemporary consumerist society and its manifestations in film, cartoons, advertising, and so forth. "Postmodernism" is fundamentally a sophisticated way of understanding consumerist-industrial society, and as such, can offer no alternative or solution to the "postmodern dilemma" because it has no purchase from outside. In order to truly critique modern society, one has to have a means of going beyond it or of seeing it from the "outside." Only metaphysics offers this possibility.

But modernity—by which I mean consumerist-industrial society—emerged in the Christian or post-Christian world after almost two millennia of very uneasy relations with those who represented what I am terming metaphysics here, but more often than not were labelled "heretics." In order to understand modernity, and how we moderns came to see nature not as sacred but as a collection of "resources," we must first look back at the long and vigorous Christian hostility to "heretics," and consider what all too often marked one as a "heretic." For I believe that the history of Western heretic-hunting is in fact symptomatic of a broader hostility to what I am terming metaphysics. Understanding heretic-hunting allows us to understand some hidden and important aspects of modernity.

Chapter Five

The Diagnosis of "Heretics"

In our preceding work *The New Inquisitions*, we saw the juridical origins of Christian heretic-hunting in antiquity. Tertullian, Irenaeus, Epiphanius, and some others—grouped under the heading of the "Ante-Nicene Fathers," who wrote in the first few centuries after Christ—saw themselves as prosecutors of the faith, as proto-inquisitors whose job was to attack those whom they perceived as "heretics." Thus we find works like *The Refutation of All Heresies* by Hippolytus—works that clearly construct a Christianity not so much in itself as by what it is claimed *not to be*. In other words, central to the foundation of confessional or historicist Christianity is not affirmation, but rejection. Central to this form of Christianity is the assertion of what is it not.

It is striking to compare the works of many of these authors, who were given the place of honor as "Fathers of the Church," with the works of those collected under the heading of the much-denigrated "Gnostics." The Gnostics spent little or no effort on attacking others, other than to note in passing that there were non-gnostics who, though they styled themselves religious, were in fact, as the Gospel of Philip puts it, "dry canals."[40] The Gnostics, by contrast, were primarily concerned with what we might call "spiritual cartography," which includes both mapping the realms beyond the physical, seen in visionary revelation, and delineating the sheer transcendence of Basilidean negative theology. Hence the Gnostic writings proliferated as the various Gnostic schools and figures outlined their visionary experiences, their ritual traditions, and their metaphysics.

It is true that Clement of Alexandria and Dionysius the Areopagite brought aspects of Gnostic traditions into what became known as the "orthodox" Christian currents. Thus, Clement argued that there is a "true gnosis" that should be acknowledged and revered within the Christian tradition, but that there is also a "false gnosis" that must be rejected. In this way, he was able to accommodate both the inquisitorial and the gnostic dimensions of Christianity. Dionysius, for his part, was a conduit through which Christianity could re-assimilate Platonic and Gnostic metaphysics, and it was by these two authors that many subsequent Christians could reassure those with an inquisitorial bent that their work was in fact not heretical.

But the fact remains that Western Christianity in particular divided itself into two broad camps, mortally opposed to one another, with only some who moved between them. It certainly was possible—as the exemplars Clement of Alexandria and Dionysius demonstrate—to have a Christianity that includes gnosis, and that nonetheless is not in conflict with the doctrines of exoteric or confessional historicist Christianity. Indeed, this is exactly what we saw in Basilides and his school, which was very early in the history of Christianity. Unfortunately, however, by the medieval period, and certainly by the time of Meister Eckhart in the thirteenth century, Inquisitional thinking, with its instinctive suspicion of "heresy," had taken a firm hold in the West. Thus, even a spiritual genius like Eckhart could not regenerate an inclusive Christianity that accepted gnosis, or that acknowledged an esoteric center to the religious tradition.

For the most part, Western Christianity (and to a considerable extent its Eastern counterparts) embraced a tradition of *diagnosis* rather than of *gnosis*. "Diagnosis," a term incorporated into medicine, derives from the Greek *diagignoskein*, from *dia*, or "apart," and *gignoskein*, or "to perceive," the whole construction having the meaning of "to distinguish or discern by setting apart." Of course, this word has at its root the essential Proto-Indo-European combination *gno-*, which gives us not only *gnosis*, but also other words in this combination, like *know*, or *cognition* or *recognition*, or even words like *cunning*. But "diagnosis" privileges a particular kind of ratiocinative knowledge, a secondary knowledge deriving from examination through comparison. *Gnosis* is the act of direct cognition itself; *diagnosis* is the secondary act of rational examination and discernment.

Certainly I am not suggesting there is no place for discernment or *diagnosis*. Rather, I am suggesting that, as we look at the trajectory of confessional Christianity over the course of the centuries, we see a juridical or prosecutorial emphasis from the Ante-Nicene Fathers onward.

This prosecutorial dimension of Christianity was institutionalized in the Inquisitions, which is the outward and most extreme manifestation of a diagnostic attitude that not only privileges the secondary act of rational examination, but also sets it directly against the primary act of gnosis or direct spiritual cognition. Instead of diagnosis and gnosis complementing one another, in much of Christianity they were turned into mortal enemies, the signs of whose combat were the torture instruments of the inquisitorial henchmen, and the pyre upon which the "heretics" were burned to death.

Now one might think that Protestantism represented a reform of Christianity, but did it? The "reformation" in fact was primarily institutional or outward, and although it had an inward dimension represented by the Christian theosophic tradition of Jacob Böhme (1575-1624), this inward dimension never sought nor did it ever take on centrality within Protestantism. Although the Böhmean theosophic current certainly represented a reawakening of gnosis within the Christian tradition, particularly in Böhme's negative theology of the *Nichts* and of the *Ungrund*, these pivotal gnostic concepts hardly took hold even within Christian theosophy itself, let alone outside it.[41] Instead, Protestantism manifested itself in such institutional movements as Lutheranism, Calvinism, Puritanism, or Anglicanism.

And what about Protestant revivalism? Don't the occasional "Great Awakenings," especially in North America, constitute a kind of new gnosis? I would argue no, on the premise that gnosis is not just anything. If we accept the idea that gnosis is characterized by negative theology as is visible in Basilides, in Meister Eckhart, and in Jacob Böhme (to name only three, but three who represent the peaks and turning points in Western Christian history) then there is little evidence of gnosis in Protestant revivalism. Rather, Protestant revivalism is characterized, from the eighteenth through the twenty-first centuries, by psychological phenomena and worldly effects—by inspired laughter, by glossolalia, by miraculous healings, by serpent-handling, by being "slain in the spirit," by evidence of wild enthusiasm. And revivalism is also often characterized or followed upon by a spirit of diagnosis—of hunting about for the signs of the devil in others, if not in oneself.

Indeed, we are hard pressed to find a single example of a Protestant gnostic, or indeed, any gnostics at all from the nineteenth century onward. One can think of only a couple of exceptions—primarily non-Protestant. One is Franklin Merrell-Wolff (1887-1985), and another is Bernadette

Roberts (1931-), both of whom are Americans who resided mostly in California. Merrell-Wolff was deeply influenced by Vedanta and especially by Buddhism, and Roberts stands firmly in the tradition of Roman Catholicism in the line of Meister Eckhart. Both are certainly seminal gnostic figures, both represent the high tradition of negative theology drawn from direct spiritual experience, but neither could accurately be described as Protestant.

What has prevailed and indeed triumphed in Western Christianity is what I am terming the "diagnostic" tradition, the one that consistently and constantly seeks to define itself by finding others whom it can paint as being "of the devil's party." Böhme himself is exemplary of this inherent tendency within Western Christianity—after he circulated his first major book, *Aurora*, on the cusp of the seventeenth century, his local Lutheran pastor (one Gregorius Richter) insisted that Böhme not publish any further works, and otherwise sought to suppress and oppose Böhme's unique spiritual genius. Böhme is an archetypal and seminal gnostic who lived the beginning of Protestantism, and it is emblematic that he was so bitterly opposed by the local Protestant pastor as well as some others in the community. Witch-hunting and heretic-hunting are not the sole province of Roman Catholicism, by any means.

The diagnostic or prosecutorial tradition within Christianity is fundamentally dualistic, and derives from what Böhme called the *turba* of the external reason. Through self-will, Böhme writes, men seek to raise up a tower of Babel, to vaunt themselves and to denigrate others (as Böhme himself had experienced). The true Christian, Böhme says, has "no controversy with the children of God." Such a one, like Böhme himself, does not condemn the views of others, but understands them inwardly—such a one only "brings them [others] to the center, and there has the proof and touchstone of all things." By contrast, the external reason seizes upon opinions and holds fast to them, attempting to build up a "Babel," not through the spirit of Christ, but by its own might alone.[42]

What Böhme suggests is very much akin to what we saw much earlier in Basilides. We will recall that Basilides was not in conflict with the exoteric Christianity of his day—from all accounts, he accepted it, but also included esoteric dimensions (in particular, his negative theology). Here again, Böhme was not in conflict with exoteric Lutheranism, but offered insight into additional inward dimensions of Christianity. Such insights emerged, he said, from his direct experiential knowledge of the center, the "proof and touchstone of all things," and his experience of the center meant that he was not in conflict with anyone because he understood all others in relation to it. This understanding is not the same as endorsement, of course.

Rather, Böhme wrote that people may live in what he termed a world of wrath or a world of love. The wrathful world is essentially demonic—it's the world of wrathful enmity or opposition. We see wrath emerging into the human world through persecutions, crimes, and wars. But there is another principle at work in the world, which Böhme likened to sap rising through the trunk and branches of a single tree. This other principle is the "effectual working love of Jesus Christ in us." For Böhme, as for Buddhism, love or compassion is identical with gnosis or direct experience of the divine. We may enter into this love-world, but do so through an inner rebirth, through an inner marriage that takes place in heaven, signifying that we become a "new man."[43]

In this new life in the spirit, Böhme tells us, we forsake our habitual concern for "body, life, honor and goods," and kindle instead our inner longing for the divine. If we are faithful to this inner call, we will experience an inward marriage with Sophia or Divine Wisdom, the inner spouse of our soul. Böhme likens his esoteric teachings to a precious pearl given him by God, a pearl to which some remain blind. Those who follow these teachings, he continues, may offend others with their simplicity, in particular offending those who "remind blind to themselves in the wisdom of their own reason." The blind "see and yet do not understand [the pearl];" they "scorn and despise the simplicity of Christ."[44] But this simplicity of the individual, and of is rooted or grounded in heaven, and its signs are a lack of concern for worldly goods and for self, and a loving care for others.

Of course, there are self-evident parallels between Gnosticism and these letters of spiritual direction from Böhme. We have already seen that both Basilides and Böhme did not see their esoteric Christianity as being inherently in conflict with exoteric Christianity. Rather, the conflict was from the side of exoteric Christianity—Richter and others opposed Böhme, just as various among the Church Fathers opposed Basilides. But the parallels go further. Böhme's discussion of the soul's inner marriage in heaven with Sophia is quite reminiscent of Valentinus's well-known emphasis on spiritual marriage and on the related symbolism of the bridal chamber. Furthermore, the "pearl of great price" referred to by Böhme is well known as a Gnostic metaphor.

But the most essential parallel is implicit. It is the parallel of gnosis itself. In the tradition that Böhme represents, Christianity is not a matter of doctrinal acquiescence, nor is it a matter of enthusiastic signs like speaking in tongues. Rather, it is an experiential and existential awakening of the individual who joins inwardly with the "tree" or body of Christ. This inward union is gnosis, expressed through the metaphor of the marriage of the soul with Sophia and of inward participation in the "nuptial joys" of heaven. Böhme is absolutely insistent that this participation is selfless. It is possible for the self to attempt to take hold of inward light for its own possession, and hold the fiery nature for itself, but this is a Luciferian effort doomed to fail.[45]

What Böhme would call a Luciferian assertion of self has to take as its implicit basis a diagnostic perspective, that is to say, it is fundamentally dualistic. Gnosis, on the other hand, refers to the realization of consciousness without an object, or alternatively put, of consciousness of awareness. This is why Dionysius, for example, refers consistently to how the Divine is "unnameable," "unutterable," "immeasurable," "unknown," and so forth.[46] This apophatic language doesn't mean that the Divine can't be known—it means, rather, that apophatic knowledge of the Divine is not expressible or understandable in dualistic subject-object or self-other terms. But the diagnostic perspective is founded in the duality of self and other, of self assessing and positioning itself in relation to other. And so its tendency is to project its own inherent dualism onto gnosis—hence the metaphors of gnosis are taken literally by diagnostic interpreters who look for signs of "dualism," and who project their own dualism upon Gnostics (who ironically represent nothing if not the transcendence of dualism).

As Böhme insists, and as the history of inquisitionalism in the West makes abundantly clear, Western Christianity has embedded within it a dualistic, "heretic"-hunting tendency.[47] Inquisitionalism is in fact an outward manifestation or institutional expression of reified diagnosticism, which Böhme calls intoxication in the *turba* of selfish reason. Gnosis, on the other hand, requires a *metanoia*, a shift into a different kind or mode of consciousness that is not self-other or subject-object. This much is clear from all of our sources, beginning with Basilides and such works as the Gospel of Thomas, all the way up through Böhme and right into the twenty-first century in an archetypal gnostic like Bernadette Roberts.[48]

Bernadette Roberts

It is noteworthy that the twentieth century did not produce many Christian mystics in the classical tradition of *via negativa*. A striking exception is the American author Bernadette Roberts (b. 1931), who once remarked that her place is "outside the traditional frame of reference—or the beaten path of mystical theology so well travelled by Christian contemplatives."[49] Here, we will look briefly at her work as a contemporary example of someone who followed an individual gnostic path. Admittedly, her work remains resolutely individualistic—it has no social, cultural, or political implications, at least not at first glance. But she does offer us a window into a particular series of inner experiences.

Roberts's writings chronicle her progressive spiritual realizations of what she came to call "no-self," and so strong are her experiences that she goes on to write that "In the Christian tradition, the falling away of self (not the ego) has never [before] been addressed!"[50] Late in her book *The Experience of No-Self*, she does recognize her deep affinity with Eckhart as "one who has made the journey [to no-self] and crossed over," and it is to his tradition as much as any that she belongs.[51] Roberts is in fact arguably the most important Christian gnostic of the past few centuries.[52]

The heart of Roberts's work, as one can quickly see, lies in her journey to and progressive realization of what she calls no-self. She outlines this journey in her book *The Experience of No-Self* (1982), and its culmination in her subsequent book *The Path to No-Self* (1985/rpt. 1991). *The Experience of No-Self* is, Roberts writes, "the personal account of a two-year journey in which I experienced the falling away of everything I can call a self. It was a journey through an unknown passageway that led to a life so new and different that, despite nearly forty years of varied contemplative experiences, I never suspected its existence."[53] In this book, her journey begins in earnest when she gazes into her empty self and discovers that she can find no self, whereupon she experiences a sensation like an elevator falling hundreds of floors. After this stunning experience, she realizes that "When there is no personal self, there is no personal God." She saw clearly that these two go together—"and where they went, I have never found out."[54]

No personal self, no personal God—by the strictest definition, Roberts's work belongs to the via negativa. What we find in the writings of Meister Eckhart, we find also in the work of Roberts—in the works of both, we encounter sheer transcendence. The difference, and this may be a particularly modern difference, is that Roberts's work is strikingly autobiographic in nature; she takes us along with her on her journey to no-self. Roberts is not interested in her antecedents, and even goes far as to suggest that to read the works of prior mystics is misguided.

The Experience of No-Self is an arresting work precisely because, unlike its antecedents in mystical literature, it is so thoroughly autobiographical. The paradox of Roberts's work is that while her subject is no-self, her narratives of her mystical experiences draw one in precisely because they are so personal. Indeed, I know of no parallel to Roberts's intensely personal accounts of her mystical journey. By "intensely personal," I do not mean that Roberts discusses her ordinary or mundane life, except in passing. We learn along the way that she had had four children, and that at the time of her breakthrough experiences, she was in her forties. But much of her early narrative takes place in the wilderness of the California mountains or along the windswept highlands of Big Sur, in solitude. Her narrative is intensely personal in that she tells us, stage by stage, experience by experience, exactly what happened in her inner life.

Roberts's works tell of her gradual and harrowing awakening to the nature of no-self, that is to say, to the deeper and deeper realization that conventional distinctions between self and other do not have any lasting or fundamental reality. Some might call this an experience of God, but Roberts is skeptical of such terms, writing that "I am always reluctant to use the word 'God,' because everybody seems to carry around their own stagnant images and definitions that totally cloud the ability to step outside a narrow, individual frame of reference."[55] Rather, she gives experiential descriptions like these:

> Initially, with the falling away of all sense of having an interior life, there had been a turning outward to the seeing of Oneness and the falling away of everything particular and individual. The seeing itself was not located within, but first seemed to be like 3D glasses imposed upon my ordinary vision, and later, localized as a seeing 'on top of the head.'[56]

She entered into what she came to call "the Great Passageway," a perilous state in which she thought she might be going insane, and though which she navigated primarily by following an inner voice that drove her forward, insisting that she must "see." It was then, she wrote that she realized "despite the coming and going of what we call life and energy, something remains that never moves nor participates in these passages. Something that is just there, just watching, and 'that' is true life, while all the energies that come and go are not true life. But what is 'that' that remains and observes?"[57]

The sequel to her first book is *Path to No-Self*, a less immediately narrative work than *The Experience of No-Self*. In *Path*, Roberts describes her experiences, but in a more abstract way, and more specifically in relation to Christ. She writes that Christ "was not involved in social work." She continues:

> I see Christ first and foremost as a mystic who had the continuous vision of God and whose mission was to share it, give it to others. Few people see it this way; instead, they have exploited Christ's good works to justify their own busy lives, lives without interior vision and therefore lives without Christ. As already said, performance of our duties and responsibilities as human beings, respect for the rights of others, lending a helping hand are what it means to be human; there is nothing particularly Christian about it.[58]

Distinctively Christian is what she terms the awakening of the "butterfly," that is, of inner spiritual vision.

This inner spiritual vision is the realization of no-self. At one point, Roberts quotes Henry Suso, and observes that all too often, someone who affirms his own "self-abandonment" in the manner of Suso is roundly condemned, perhaps even crucified, because "unwittingly, he is saying that he is a man without sin!" But in reality, "a man without a self is not about to stand up and say 'I have no sin.' He cannot say this because the truth of the matter is: he has no 'I.'"[59] We can see here how Roberts runs up against what we may call confessional Christian theological fears. The realization of no-self doesn't mean the absence of sins; it means that there is in reality an absence of *I*. But from a conventional, dualistic Christian perspective, such an assertion is frightening, not least because it implies that there is no permanent self, no enduring entity that is to inherit heaven.

On reflection, we can see here what Roberts is alluding to: it is the implicit conflict between dualistic conventional understandings, or perhaps more accurately from her perspective, misunderstandings of Christianity on the one hand, and the realization of the unitive state or or no-self on the other. The confessional understanding of Christ: he was an historical figure who lived and died in order that he might vicariously bear our sins and bring forgiveness to us. Thus *I* am to discover a *personal* relationship with *him*. But Roberts freely admits that she was never able to discern the *personality* of Christ. Rather, she says, Christ's presence in the Eucharist and in us is mystical, and we must meet him on this "deep, hidden, unknown, and inexpressible" level. For "Christ is not the self, but that which remains when there is no self." Christ is "the act, the manifestation and extension of God that is not separate from God. We cannot comprehend 'that' which acts or 'that' which smiles, but we all know the act—the smile that is Christ himself."[60]

When one looks closely at her work, and in particular its central theme of realizing one's absence of any substantive self, one has to think of Buddhism, and indeed, she did spend at least a week with Zen Buddhist contemplatives.[61] She cheerfully admits, in a third book *What is Self?*, that it is in Buddhism she found the clearest references to what she had experienced, the experiences of transcending ego and of no-self, or in Japanese, *kensho* and *satori*. But she insists that Buddhism and for that matter Vedanta are not central influences for her; she is indeed a Christian contemplative. What she does not acknowledge so readily is that her antecedents in the Christian tradition are figures like Dionysius, Eckhart, and the author of the *Cloud*, or that she belongs to the longstanding tradition of the *via negativa*. Perhaps this is because her narrative is so profoundly intimate—it is a chronicle of her own experiences, and while intellectually, the *via negativa* tradition is clearly precedent, it does not offer the kind of personal accounts that she does. In fact, I know of no comparable personal accounts of awakening experiences in the literature of Buddhism or Christianity.

The works of Bernadette Roberts remind us of what we could call a classical American tradition that emphasizes or privileges direct individual experience. This tradition is inaugurated by the nineteenth-century American Transcendentalists, notably Ralph Waldo Emerson, Henry David Thoreau, and Bronson Alcott, and is visible also in William James's *Varieties of Religious Experience*.[62] I do not want to overemphasize the American dimensions of Roberts's work—she is after all in the classical European mystical tradition that stretches from Dionysius the Areopagite through Meister Eckhart and the *Cloud of Unknowing*, a *via negativa* tradition that belongs to no language, people, or nation. I only wish to note that Roberts nonetheless exists within an American tradition too, one that insists on the primacy of direct individual spiritual experience over secondary or comparative constructs. Furthermore, she is clearly a gnostic, in contradistinction to the confessional Christian diagnostic tradition.

But is gnosis a purely individual affair? Is it possible that there might be political implications? If so, what would they be? We have seen the importance of negative theology already as the most natural expression for the inexpressibility of gnosis. But the political, or socio-political implications of gnosis at least to my knowledge have never been explored. Let us then turn our attention to what a gnostic politics would look like.

Chapter Six

The Political Implications of Gnosis

As we have already seen, there is a considerable body of anti-gnostic polemics, to which the twentieth century unfortunately contributed its share. More than one author, indeed at times it seems a kind of cottage industry constructed a variety of fantasies about Gnostics and their supposedly pernicious effect on politics over the millennia.[63] But such fantasies bear no relation to Gnostic texts or groups in late antiquity, or to the metaphysical dimensions of gnosis that we have been outlining thus far. Rather, "Gnosticism" to these polemicists—indebted as they are to the heresiophobic Church Fathers like Tertullian—is merely a floating signifier, an inchoate clot of mud that serves chiefly to smear on one's political enemies. Yet the question thus arises: if we were to take seriously the idea of gnosis, what would its political or socio-political consequences be? It is not so difficult to envision a gnostic community as one might at first think.

Gnosis and the Human Community

Let us begin, then, not with useless and ungrounded polemics, but with the metaphysical premises inherent in gnosis as expressed in the apophatic tradition exemplified by the Basilidean current. If gnosis is best expressed through negation, what would be the political and theological consequence of that negation? Here, at the outset, we have already leapt ahead to the heart of the matter. For negative theology by its very nature is a refusal of ideological or theological dogmatism; it is a rejection of formulaic expression and simultaneously a recognition that although language may express and awaken the experience of gnosis, language also serves as a mask, or even as an eclipse of the experience within. Negative theology is, then, by its very nature a refusal of ideocracy.

Thus a gnostic community necessarily would be cautious about doctrinal constructions, and would be aware of the dangers of sectarianism. Historically, this is in fact precisely what we see when we look at the history of figures from Basilides to Meister Eckhart or to the author of the *Cloud of Unknowing*, or to the school of Jacob Böhme, or for that matter to Bernadette Roberts in the early twenty-first century. In all of these cases, we note that these gnostics, who belong to the *via negativa* tradition, established no sect with an organizational structure, no church, no ecclesiastical body. It is true that they each *influenced* subsequent gnostics, as for instance Eckhart influenced Johannes Tauler—he represented an aspirational example. This is the legacy of the gnostic, which is analogous to the legacy of the Christ who asked others to follow him.

An exception, one might argue, is Jacob Böhme (1575-1624), who inspired a long tradition of Christian theosophers after him, including gnostics like John Pordage (1608-1681), as well as the more speculative intellectual approach of Franz von Baader (1765-1841). But here too, we see no founding of a Böhmean sect or church. Indeed, Böhme's works include very clear denunciations of sectarianism and dogmatic constructs that act as a barrier to direct spiritual experience and inner awakening. Böhme denigrated what he termed "Babel," meaning an organizational church or sect that insisted on outward acquiescence in doctrine or outward practices without any inner or spiritual life to invigorate them. Böhme emphasized that one must undergo spiritual awakening for oneself, and at the center of this awakening is the realization of what he, and Pordage after him, termed the *Ungrund*, or "not-ground," and the *Nichts*, or the Divine Nothing.

By contrast, when the English mystic Jane Leade (1623-1704) sought to found a proselytizing organization, the Philadelphian Society, around the turn of the eighteenth century, she was roundly condemned by European theosophers for precisely this reason: in so doing, she was attempting to make theosophy over into an organizational structure with doctrinal constructs. It is interesting to note that Leade was not in the *via negativa* tradition. A visionary, most of her works consist in her recounting of her spectacular visionary experiences with the Virgin Sophia, for instance, envisioned as a celestial being—without much hint of the *Ungrund* or the *Nichts* that were so central for Böhme and Pordage, for instance. Thus, Leade quite arguably does not fully belong to the theosophic tradition—she represents, rather, a visionary dimension separated from the *via negativa* that consistently informs the visionary dimensions of Böhme's or Pordage's works.

Now this is very much the critique of Leade leveled by an almost exactly contemporary theosopher, Johann Georg Gichtel (1638-1710). Gichtel, known as "the hermit of Amsterdam," co-edited the first full edition of the works of Böhme, entitled *Theosophia Revelata*, so it is very clear that he knew his Böhme. But more important for us is his collection of personal letters, which were published under the title *Theosophia Practica*. In those letters, Gichtel discussed Leade and her Philadelphian Society at some length. Initially, he was not sure what to make of her, but in time, he came to the view that she had succumbed to what in theosophy is termed the *spiritus mundi*, or Spirit of this World. It is quite important to understand this concept of *spiritus mundi*, because in theosophy it is seen as a primary blocking mechanism or barrier to our freedom.

The *spiritus mundi*, although it is personalized or anthropomorphized often in Gichtel's letters, is in fact at least in part a psychological principle. It can be understood as the psychological principle of worldly distraction or attachment, and it works in the following way: it encourages attachment, in particular, to fixed ideas. Those fixed ideas might be of the accumulation of wealth or of possessions; or they might be a set of abstract doctrines for which an individual may become outwardly ascetic. What matters is the mechanism: our fixation generates a kind of hardened psychological "shell" or "carapace" with which we can identify, and which buttresses our sense of personal identity. The *spiritus mundi* works on an individual level, but it also can be seen in collectives.

When Leade sought to create an organized Philadelphian Society, she was moving the group of London theosophers toward the creation of a sect. Sects are formed around fixed doctrines and ideas with which people identify, and that reinforce the individual's sense of self. This is, of course, in direct contrast to the *via negativa* tradition that points us toward the transcendence of self and other; the *spiritus mundi* inclines us toward selfish identification with a set of ideas that are *ours*, as opposed to *them*. Thus the theosophers who understood this psychological mechanism were highly critical of sectarianism, because their aim was to encourage penetration beyond it, beyond what Gichtel termed an "astral shell."

"Astral shell" is a fairly straightforward idea with a great deal of explanatory power, especially for cult or sect formation. The theosophers were critical of the sects of their time, including groups like the Quakers, which theosophers like Gichtel criticized as having built up an ideological "shell" that cut them off from more profound spiritual progress. Attachment to the sectarian label, and an attachment to worldly life, meant that the sect members formed a kind of inner barrier to ascent, and the barrier itself becomes the basis for the group's identity—thus, to leave the sect is inherently to lose part of one's personal identity. One is trapped as if inside an invisible "shell" or force field.

But let us take some a more modern example of what is often termed a "cult." What is attractive about a cult or sectarian new religious movement? It is true that there is often a charismatic leader, but the leader alone is not enough to form a cohesive group. What's necessary is to build up a group adherence to a set of ideas or doctrines that sets the group apart from society as a whole and offers members a special new identity. As the group leader and members construct their doctrinal identity, they build a kind of inner shell that separates them from other human beings, and in extreme cases, they build a shell so adamantine that they begin to believe in their own superiority over other people, even in their own "authorization" as *Übermensch* to commit inhuman acts, to extort or kill. We saw exactly this in a group like Aum Shinrikyo, which actually set off poison gas in a crowded Tokyo subway, and which in addition to creating biological weapons, sought to purchase nuclear weapons.

The process by which a group forms a psychological shell is the exact reverse of gnosis. Gnosis is the process of going beyond the self-other division into what is often termed negative theology but could perhaps more accurately be termed negative theosophy—it is the process of transcendence. By contrast, a cult or for that matter a political ideology works in precisely the reverse way: it intensifies the self-other division by emphasizing *us* against *them*. This descent into dualism results in heretic-hunting or scapegoating because the vilified "other" is necessary for group identity. As Carl Schmitt's "political theology" had it, the world must be divided into "friends" and "enemies." A political religion, or a religious politics, requires a distinguishing ideology to which adherents can fiercely cling, and it requires scapegoats or heretics to further define the reigning ideology. To create these two—ideology and scapegoats—is to create an "astral" or psychological shell. Such a shell is, of course, individual, but it also belongs to and is reinforced by a group identity.

Once we understand this dynamic of carapace generation, and once we understand how it functions in human society, we can see also what its reverse is—that is, the deconstruction of ideology and, concurrently, of self-reinforcing dualistic identity. This deconstruction (if we may so put it) is visible in the *via negativa* current that we see from Basilides to Eckhart, and from Böhme to Roberts, that is, all the way from the very early Christian era up to the twenty-first century. The *via negativa*, as Roberts's narrative makes quite clear from an experiential or first-hand perspective, is the progressive shedding of self-other illusions and the progressive movement into the mystery of transcendence. In relation to human community, the *via negativa* means—to begin with—relinquishing our ideological clinging; it means *letting go*.

Paradoxically, this *letting go* or *gelassenheit*, although it has great implications for human community, is an individual endeavor that takes place in solitude. Each must go through this door alone. We see this profound solitude exemplified for us in the loneliness of Christ in the wilderness and in the solitary meditating Buddha; and we see it also in those who evidence great caution concerning sectarian or doctrinal/ideological constructs. Thus Buddhism belongs to the *sangha*, that is, to all who follow in the path of the Buddha. What we see—in the fragments of Basilides and in the gnomic sermons of Eckhart, in the voluminous works of Böhme and in the *Cloud of Unknowing* as well as in the narratives of Bernadette Roberts—is advice on following a particular path, a path not of clinging but of letting go.

Now we begin to see more clearly and from a different perspective the nature of modern politics. Politics is persuasion and coercion of the masses, something that became even more visible in the era of mass media. In its most extreme form, modern mass political life manifested itself in totalitarianism, in the mass rallies of National Socialism and in the grandiose parades of the Soviets and the Chinese. But even more generally, modern political life consists in the shaping of mass opinion through slogans and emotional manipulation using nationalism or patriotism as an emotional fuel. Modern politics is fundamentally about organizing society in ways that maximize the wealth and power of an authoritarian elite, and modern political life functions via the collective construction of an astral or psychological shell.

Gnosis, on the other hand, represents an individual path toward independence from such conditioning. It is not that gnostic life is aimed at the dismantling of political or social expectations, but rather that the gnostic path inherently entails an indifference to politico-economic power. On reflection, we can see why this naturally would be so. The gnostic path is concerned primarily with inward life, not with control over others or with notions of reshaping the human world in one's own image. What would be the point? What matters, rather, is living a virtuous life, that is, living a life without outward conflicts, a life conducive to interior vision and illumination. Such a life is not only indifferent to the accumulation of power, but also increasingly beyond past or habitual social conditioning.

If it is true that the gnostic is otherworldly, such otherworldliness does not translate into a desire to reshape this world. Indeed, totalitarian despots in the twentieth century from Lenin and Hitler to Mao and Pol Pot all sought to reshape this world—all were hostile to traditional religion and believed that, with sufficient social upheaval and mass murder, they could create a new society, even a new humanity. By contrast, one cannot find a single gnostic in history that sought such aims. The greatest evil in the twentieth century was wrought by those whose worlds were bounded by the horizon of history, for whom this world and its reshaping is all, and inner or visionary life mean nothing. By contrast, the gnostic, whose aim is transcendence of self-and-other dichotomy, is indifferent to this-worldly power. Was it not Christ who said that his kingdom is not of this world?

What then might a gnostic polity look like? Without doubt, it would be a polity with an ethos of live and let live, an ethos based in individual freedom and responsibility, a polity akin to those we see occasionally in antiquity or during the medieval or early modern periods, when it was possible for small groups to live apart and devote themselves to the inner life. One thinks, for example, of the small community surrounding John Pordage during the middle of the seventeenth century. Around them was the turbulence of England during a period of civil war, yet Pordage and his circle lived in reclusion, and were not caught up in external events, for what mattered was their interior life—the visionary experiences and illumination that he chronicled in his books.

A gnostic polity is a small community of like-minded souls, unconcerned with what others do because they are more concerned with removing the mote from their own eye than with looking after the log in their neighbor's. They live simple lives, close to nature, in Pordage's case, practicing herbal medicine, tending a garden, and, when possible, caring for those less fortunate than themselves. It is no accident that, in all the writings of those in Pordage's small circle during his lifetime, we find no trace of historical events; theirs are the chronicles of visionary experiences, their important events those that took place on a visionary inner horizon—the illuminations of divine Wisdom. Imagine a society comprised of a number of such small communities, each devoted to virtuous and contemplative life. What manner of culture would that be?

Such a culture would have far less impact on the natural world than modern society does. The profligate waste of warfare would not happen; one would not see the slow warfare on nature that industrial society wages. We would see more cottage industry and handcraft, more farming and artisanal work, the kinds of labor that conduce to contemplative life. What, after all, are the cultural values that orient us? If a community is oriented toward contemplative or inner life, this has major implications for its organization and activities. Family and community life are oriented around and illuminated by a contemplative center, and as a result society is inclined toward much greater stability than is a society oriented outwardly toward exploitation of the human and natural worlds.

An exploitive approach to others is, after all, inherently dualistic—it inevitably means that *I* seek control over *them* or over *it*. Human relationships are seen in terms of usefulness to oneself primarily; there is little or no sense of commonality beyond the merely instrumental. By contrast, a gnostic approach to others has as its underlying premise one's inherent unity with them by virtue of the *via negativa*, that is to say, by virtue of the self-transcendence that is beyond both "I" and "thou." Of course, "a gnostic approach to others" does not refer to a fixed state, but to an orientation or inclination—a direction of intent. This underlying intent informs, indeed, generates culture, that is, a communal orientation toward care for others, but ultimately toward realizing the transcendence of self-other dualism.

Historically, there are instances of such communities, but by their very nature they tend to be decentralized and to be almost invisible in the chronicles of wars, seizures of power, and other events that usually are termed history. We can see such groups in the early Christian Gnostics, and again in medieval sects like the Friends of God, as well as in the circle around John Pordage in mid-seventeenth century England. But in all of these cases, such groups lived in a hostile ambience—Pordage was falsely charged with a variety of misdemeanors by his fellow ministers, and in reply asked "And now ye Ministers of *Berks*, my persecutors, tell me, what wrong or injury have I done you; have I lusted to preach in any of your Pulpits? Have I privately gone from parish to parish, or from house to house to get followers, or make proselites of your hearers? Have I publicly or privately railed against you or your Doctrines? . . . Why then am I persecuted with so much fury, and violence, as though I were not worthy to live amongst you?" And his most revealing point of all: "Have I not lived privately in my own place, onely holding forth that strict, dying, resigning life, as the way to life eternal[?]"[64]

Pordage and his circle, like the various predecessor groups, sought to live in reclusion engaged in contemplative praxis, but he was tried on false charges and driven from the ministry. Earlier, medieval groups were under the constant threat of the Inquisition and of the dreadful penalties for "heresy," and even in the comparative freedom from the Inquisition of early modern England, Pordage was harshly criticized and punished for what, in the end, was simply his desire to live "privately in my own place, onely holding forth that strict, dying, resigning life, as the way to life eternal." When we look at Pordage's reclusive life as a whole, we cannot help but be impressed at his devotion on the one hand to feeding, clothing, and healing others, and on the other to contemplative and visionary praxis as detailed in his extensive writings. Although Pordage was a visionary, at the center of his work was what Böhme termed the *Ungrund* and the *Nichts* or Nothing, and Pordage ultimately belonged to the larger current of via negativa mysticism. One wonders what his community might have been like if they had existed in a socially supportive ambience. What form would such a larger community have taken?

The point here is that we have very few pre-modern or early modern examples of gnostic groups or circles integrated into a larger society and engaged in mutual cross-pollination or cross-fertilization with it. Rather, such groups have for the most part been depicted as rebellious even if, as Pordage's eloquent response to his persecutors makes clear, they were not rebels but simply wanted to live free to practice their contemplative pursuits. This opposition between gnostic individuals or groups and society as a whole is not a given—rather, it emerges because of an underlying opposition in metaphysical orientation. The gnostic groups are oriented toward transcendence of self and other; the non-gnostic society as a whole is oriented toward dualism, that is, toward a self-other dichotomy. Were this broad distinction to be overcome, were a gnostic group to exist within a supportive society, what might the larger result look like? In order to understand this, we must look again at nature, but this time, at nature as part of a larger polity.

Gnosis and the Community of Nature

The language of industrial society is deeply imbued with the anti-values of dualistic manipulation and exploitation of the natural world. Those who recognize this clearly then tend toward the opposite end of the spectrum, that is, toward extreme antimodernism and a rejection of all of industrial society and, in the most extreme forms, in the rejection of language and of humanity itself. These forms of extremism are visible in such figures as Theodore Kaczynski and Derrick Jensen who, in their zeal to protect nature, go so far as to endorse individualized warfare against industrial society, thus unconsciously mirroring in themselves what they detest in the other. But it is possible to go beyond these Siamese twins of modernism/antimodernism, and that is our aim here in considering what I term the community of nature.

The usual terms are "ecology" and "environmentalism," but in reality these words reveal some profound underlying misconceptions. The words embody a deep confusion. The term "ecology" derives from the Greek *oikos*, meaning "house" and, of course, the word *logos*, sometimes translated as "word." Fundamentally related to "economy," "ecology" also describes an artificial structure, that is to say, a human dwelling. However, in fact the community of nature is not *oikos* but rather *bios*, and hence the French term *bionomique* or "bionomics" became the European counterpart of economics. This is more accurate, obviously—it is very much what authors like Kaczynski or Jensen or organizations like Earth Liberation Front [ELF] are defending, that is, wilderness and the biological world beyond or outside the city walls, that is, beyond the realm of human artifice.

There is a risk in using a term like "bionomy" or "bionomics," of course, even though such words are more precise than the nebulous "ecology." The risk with bionomy or bionomics is that it becomes the functional equivalent of economics, that is to say, a different kind of manipulation of the natural world, based on the dualism that underlies industrial society and the economic theories that justify it. Very much the same risk for that matter is visible in bionomic extremism, that is, in those who insist so much on the preservation of wilderness and of nature as to be willing to wage war on their fellow humans. These antimoderns are if anything even more dualistic, since their enemy is industrial society. We must be aware of and seek to go beyond dualistic language that divides us from one another and from nature.

The term "community of nature" is, of course, essentially a translation of *bionomique*, but it no longer carries the rationalist coldness of
"bionomics." A "community of nature" is just that—communal, a shared
endeavor, and cannot be reduced to a set of manipulable parts. A community of which one is a part bears within it a non-objectifiable dimension—one *belongs* to it. To put it another way, a community of nature is
not merely an "I" and "it," or even an "I" and "thou" relationship, for it
has a dimension that goes beyond dualism. There is a community, a third,
communal dimension that transcends the division between the two. If
the term "bionomy" could carry the connotation of communion, then
it would be acceptable, but in truth, it probably cannot.

This third, transcendent dimension is expressed well by *communion*.
Intangible, perhaps even inexplicable, nonetheless it is communion that
pervades community and makes it a union and not merely a group of
parts. When we have lived our whole lives in a small town or in a rural
community, we are a part of it, and what it is goes beyond the sum of
our parts. So too, many and perhaps all of us have experienced a communion with the natural world in which we commune with it, are part
of it, our own consciousness invigorated, mysteriously enlivened by it.
And it is possible that it is also enlivened and invigorated by our own
consciousness—perhaps there is in this communion a participation and
even a mutual exchange. That is possible.

Some of the English and German Romantics, notably Blake, Wordsworth, Goethe, and Novalis recognized this communion, and in the early
modern period we see this in what is sometimes termed the cult of the
sublime. The word "sublime" implies an experience of self-transcendence
in wilderness, and we see this in the poetry of Wordsworth and in the
works of Novalis especially. It is not the case that Romanticism represented escapism from nascent industrial society—rather, it represented
the recognition, among the poets, of what was being suppressed and lost
in the human community during the early phase of industrialism. They
sought to raise high the banner of the sublime, to call attention to the
experiences of self-transcendence that are possible in wild nature, to point
out not only that we come "trailing clouds of glory," but also that a kind
of nascent gnostic recovery from ratiocentric technicism (that is, from
the "Satanic mills" of industrialism-rationalism) is possible in nature.

I say "nascent" recovery because it would be naïve to think that
simply going off into nature is itself sufficient. The Romantics—like the
back-to-nature movements in early twentieth-century Germany, and

again in the 1960s, especially in North America and Europe—although well intentioned, did not represent for the most part any particular inner discipline. Rather, by and large they represented the recognition that industrial society, for all its technical success, also meant not only separation from nature, but also inner loss and fragmentation. The return to nature is part of the healing process, but it is not in itself sufficient, and we see this reflected in the history of groups like The Farm in Tennessee, a hippie community gathered around the charismatic figure Stephen, and that over the course of decades became an exemplar of organic farm agritourism.

However laudable, back-to-nature movements, like backpacking expeditions or survivalist ventures in the wilderness, are premonitory rather than exemplary of what I am suggesting by the term "community of nature." What I am suggesting here goes significantly beyond simply entering into the wild or living off the land—it represents, rather, nothing less than the re-orientation and transformation of consciousness. It is not enough to carry into the wilderness the dualistic or alienated mentality of industrial consumerism—that mentality has to soften and begin to transform into an I-thou relationship, a sense that the hawk, the deer, the sparrow, the wildcat, the chipmunk, the oak, the running water and the wind, the soil all are present and aware in ways that we become conscious of only to the extent that we leave our dualistic, manipulative or instrumentalist mentality behind.

We begin to understand this more ancient consciousness in moments of illumination, when the barrier between "I" and "it" imperceptibly is erased by "I" and "thee," and in turn becomes invisible. This more ancient consciousness is sometimes termed nature mysticism, but that does not quite do justice to it because such a term assumes that we are subsumed into nature, or absorbed into a panglossian unity. Instead, we might consider whether gnosis is insight into that which is inherent in nature, in humanity, and in the divine—what Plotinus termed the One. Whether we term this insight the One, or as Jacob Böhme did, the *Nichts* or Nothing, we must confront beyond the terminology its unitary and inexpressible nature.

Yet we in the West are unconsciously conditioned by the fundamental dualism inhering in the monotheistic traditions, and so powerful is this dualism that monotheistic ideologues project it outward, claiming it as a primary characteristic of their "heretical" enemies. This dualism is implicit in the notion that the divine is either wholly transcendent, utterly beyond nature, or inherent in nature and thus not transcendent at all.

75

Both notions are exaggerations that derive from the divisive and misleading dimensions of monotheism. The mystical traditions of Christianity, Judaism, and Islam, are engaged in a perpetual combat with monotheistic dualism, to which nature mysticism is not a solution but a reaction.

I am pointing here well beyond what is usually termed "ecological" or "environmental" thinking, and beyond "nature mysticism" as well, toward the underlying necessity for a turning about in the deepest seat of consciousness. It is not a question of whether such a shift is possible—we know from the history of Taoism, Buddhism, Sufism, Kabbalah, and gnostic Christianity that it is. Gnostics in the West so often have moved outward into the wilderness because in doing so they can be born again, that is, they can progressively leave behind their social conditioning and slowly enter into a new world, or to put it another way, they can pass the burning sword and reënter Eden. There they can experience Edom, that is, the vitality of pure life in the wild, which prefigures and, in a premonitory sense, is liberation.

Here, of course, I refer to the eremitic life devoted to gnosis, but the fact is that many who live close to the natural world, who experience rural life, are familiar with prefigurations of a deeper inner life. Those prefigurations come unexpectedly in those moments when we experience the union of life in nature with the vital life of Edom, that is, the awakening of our inner sense that there is something archetypal beyond what we see, in what we see. This sense of the living and unearthly archetype within its earthly manifestation is what we recognize in Paleolithic cave drawings of ten millennia ago. Some awareness in us stirs with the inchoate recognition that there is spirit alive in the deer before us, and that it lives also in a community of the spirit.

In the process of urbanization and industrialization, the community of the spirit has become remote and unfamiliar, but it is nonetheless intimately present when we turn to look, or when it is awakened in us. I am not referring to the atavistic wild furies of barbarism, although they are also present and not that far from the surface either, particularly in mobs. The crowd mentality so characteristic of modernity shuts out the natural world, and fellow humanity; it blinds us to others and to the living world; the crowd mentality is an intoxication of absence, a species of madness in that a member of a mob is quite literally out of his own mind. By contrast, the community of the spirit is experienced individually and in stillness, as the presence of living inner knowledge.

What I am suggesting here, in other words, is that nature mysticism in itself is not enough—that is, communion with *natura naturalis* is not enough. One could even go so far as to suggest that nature mysticism does not really exist—rather, there is the possibility of gnosis in nature. Union with nature exists only in the context of union with what transcends nature, with what informs and may be seen through it. The community of nature is not merely what is visible, let alone what may be measured or divided. Its most important dimensions, as the Paleolithic cave images tell us, are not the visible but the invisible.

Yet the industrial and technical apparatus of modernity, for all its incredible prowess of manipulation and exploitation, exists by excluding those invisible dimensions of nature, not to mention even the concept of gnosis. The more one is immersed in one of these two perspectives, the more the other begins to fade away, like one of those clever composite images wherein one may see either one figure or another, depending on one's focus. Thus, those who are wholly immersed in a technical vision see a wooded landscape in terms of its potential for economic exploitation; whereas those who are attuned to its intangible dimensions are incapable of understanding how anyone could destroy that wooded landscape for lucre.

The community of nature, in other words, is the community of the visible and the invisible or to put it another way, of the tangible and the intangible, of the living, and of the ancestors. When we are immersed in the crowd-noise of modernity—which includes the myriad electronic forms of entertaining distraction—we are to that extent forgetful of this other community. Indeed, we might suggest that a primary function of electronic distractions is to offer a substitute for the more ancient communities to which we naturally belong. We forget—because we do not easily see and are so often distracted from—the invisible generations that have gone before us, and we no longer recognize them as being present or as also having a place in the community of nature. Having forgotten the past, we have forgotten also the future, and the link between the two. To belong to the community of nature is to recognize not only those we see, but also those we don't see, yet who are also present.

By this I refer not only to human generations, but also to the generations of animals, of plants, including ancient trees, of fish and of birds, and of rocks, minerals, fire, earth, water, and sky, of landscape. It is possible that all of these also live in dimensions ordinarily invisible to us, but nonetheless present in our world, that in some sense the ancient generations of all living beings have not vanished but are present to us, especially at certain times of the year and in numinous places. Certainly that is the perception of many indigenous peoples, and it is what we see depicted in those images upon cave walls ten, twelve, or fifteen millennia ago.

Gnosis is often portrayed as anti-worldly knowledge, as the negation of nature and of the generational world. But if gnosis is, as Plotinus had it, union with the One, then the very term carries with it the implication of ultimate inclusivity. This is one of the fundamental problems of understanding gnosis in the West: it has for so long been depicted as anti-nature, anti-generational, whereas in fact it is better understood as union with that which includes and transcends nature and its invisible communities. This is what we see in the Nag Hammadi Gnostic texts, where gnosis is likened to marriage and to generation precisely because it includes and transcends those dimensions of human and natural life.

This is vitally important because what we are discussing is the path to a more complete way of understanding how we participate in the full community of nature. "Ecology," even "nature mysticism" cannot convey the kind of intensification and widening of consciousness that is expressed by the term "gnosis." Gnosis, in this context, is revolutionary in opening up entirely different ways of understanding both the human community and the larger community of nature. This is because it represents a penetration beyond the visible and beyond ratiocinative, dualistic consciousness, into new, more inclusive ways of understanding the nature world as an intergenerational community of the visible and the invisible. Gnosis is not reducible to seeing or conversing with spirits, or to other visionary experiences. But it is possible, is it not, that gnosis may include such dimensions of human experience?

If this is so, then we begin to understand more clearly why gnosis has political and bionomic implications. It includes the visionary realization of communities that ordinarily remain veiled to us, and as such it points us toward recognizing how the timeless is visible within time. The word "gnosis" represents the opening of an inner cartography, and it may be only in light of this inner cartography that new kinds of politico-social organization can be understood aright. Without it, the human community is limited chiefly to oneself or, perhaps, to one's immediate family, that is, to self-interest, and nature is a collection of objects to be exploited. With it, both the human and the natural communities, and all that they represent, are much greater than we saw before.

To understand more clearly why this is so, we must consider what lies beyond the horizon of history.

Chapter Seven

Beyond the Horizon of History

Historicity is the bane of our era. By "historicity," I do not mean historical awareness, of course, but rather the belief that all meaning is situated
within history alone. Such a belief is ubiquitous in our era, and is especially
strong in the West. Historicist Christianity, which after all has its origins
in Jewish messianism, perpetually has anticipated a millennial period
just ahead. Historicist millenarianism, sometimes termed "dispensational
millennialism," became endemic within American evangelical Christianity at the end of the twentieth century, and also was visible in Marxism
and in National Socialism and its expectation of a coming "Third Reich."
Historicism is the fundamental characteristic of secular modernity—it is
effectively the atmosphere within which moderns exist—and almost no
one considers what may be beyond the horizon of history. That is what
we will begin to explore here.

But before we explore what may be beyond history's horizon, we
must first consider a bit more the nature of the horizon itself. Secular
modernity represented, particularly in the seventeenth and eighteenth
centuries, a gradual turning-away from the possibilities of transcendence
in the West. We can see, during the early modern period, the remarkable efflorescence in Western Europe of esoteric mystico-magical and
magico-mystical traditions like alchemy. Indeed, this was the heyday of
alchemical treatises and images, within which nature was regarded as
transparent, as conveying and reflecting the divine light. Furthermore,
a great many of these alchemical treatises are in fact also mystical treatises—they directly point toward eternity, that is, toward the gnostic
transcendence of history.

By the end of the eighteenth century, these esoteric treatises were diminishing in number, and in the nineteenth century, they mostly disappear. In the late nineteenth and twentieth centuries, one finds almost no instances of *via negativa* mysticism in the West (with a couple of noteworthy exceptions like Wolff and Roberts), much less in the way of alchemy, virtually no Christian theosophy in the tradition of Böhme (again, with one or two noteworthy exceptions like Berdyaev). Esoteric religious possibilities—which had been so foregrounded in the early modern period in theosophy, in pansophy, and in alchemy—by the twentieth century were almost totally marginalized. This marginalization was the necessary result of what one may term rationalist technicism, or scientific industrialism. Traditions like alchemy are fundamentally non-dualist in that they are based in a profound union between the human, the natural, and the divine. It was necessary, indeed, inevitable that non-dualist gnostic traditions be rejected, as a fundamentally dualistic, technicist consciousness became prevalent.

Seen from this perspective, secular modernity is, at base, the result of the anti-esoteric, inquisitional mentality that governed so much of Western Christendom. The Inquisitors longed to eliminate, by intimidation and force, virtually all traces of gnosis from Christian society—and as it turns out, that is in fact what we mostly see during the early modern and modern periods. A secular, technical mentality is what one ends up with when a dualistic, strictly historicist mentality is enforced over a period of several millennia. Further evidence of this broad set of tendencies is, of course, the secular millennialism that impelled twentieth-century ideocratic dictatorships as represented by both communism and fascism—they too included fundamentally anti-esoteric, inquisitorial tendencies, and they were often (as in the cases of Communist Russia and China) militantly secular and anti-religious.

What I'm suggesting here is this: secular modernity is characterized by the constrained temporal horizon that corresponds to the hard subject-object division of technicism. By and large, a technicist, dualistic perspective is noteworthy not for what it includes as much as for what it excludes—in particular, gnosis, meaning direct individual insight into the transcendence of the subject-object division. There are, of course, authors and artists who sought to point toward or even to re-awaken such possibilities—one thinks of Berdyaev—but they are far from the mainstream and strangely ignored in the history of philosophy or literature. In other words, those who spoke for the transcendence of the subject-object division are themselves excluded from mainstream history. Also excluded, of course, are topics—the "occult" and the "mystical" became especially *outré*.

An underlying assumption of modern ideologies is the primacy of the historical: we cannot even conceive easily of what might be on the other side of an historical horizon. Millennialism is deeply embedded in new religious movements: some expect UFOs or aliens to descend to save them at the "end of time," while others expect an "Eschaton" or a Teilhardian "omega point" in history, prefigured by hallucinogen-generated visions, and still others, millenarian evangelicals, expect an elaborate historical drama of "rapture" and the historical manifestation of what are conceived as the historical prophecies of the Book of Revelation. Marxist-inspired faiths like communism and fascism are fundamentally millennialist in nature, looking forward to some imagined millenarian culmination in history. And we might recall that in the early twenty-first century, the Bush, Jr. administration and various "neoconservatives" also proposed a millenarian vision of spreading "democracy" by force around the globe.

But what is on the other side of the historical horizon? After all, the very notion of horizon is situational: it is our horizon because we are situated where it is the horizon we see, but from a more universal perspective, we are on a point on a globe, surrounded by space. A horizon, in other words, is situational and not absolute. So it is with the temporal horizon, which is relative to our perspective. We do not think about what may be beyond that horizon, for we take for granted where we are and what we see. However, that has not always been the case. In cultures informed by traditions like Buddhism, Taoism, Hinduism, Judaism, Christianity, Islam, or shamanism, we see an awareness of dimensions of human life beyond the temporal horizon. Indeed, to remind us of the supratemporal is arguably the very purpose of religion.

In the writings of an early seventeenth-century figure like John Pordage, we begin to glimpse what is encompassed under the term "supratemporal." We have already noted the kind of reclusive life of Pordage and his small community—he devoted himself to contemplation, while he outwardly served as a physician, and while he and his community supported and cared for the poor. There is, then, not a great deal further to observe about Pordage's daily life, for the many volumes of his writings include almost nothing on it. Their focus, rather, is on the inner life. If we may put it this way, Pordage went through a portal into what he termed "eternal nature," and his works consist in his accounts of what he found there, in eternity.

The word "eternity" is often objectified as a theological concept that somehow "places" eternity outside time. But, drawing on Pordage's work, it would be more accurate to see eternity as surrounding time, in the way that the earth and its atmosphere is surrounded by space. Eternity is the space in which we live, and time is our localized atmosphere. Here we see the original meaning of the word "rapture" restored: the word refers not to some bizarre and fantastic historical dramatic fiction (in which ordinary people's physical bodies magically disappear, often with imagined disastrous physical consequences like plane or automobile crashes[!]), but rather to a contemplative raptness, an inner translation into transcendent states of consciousness that are accessible to us even as we exist in time. Pordage writes that he is taken up, or translated inwardly into the "globe of eternity." The globe of eternity is another term for the divine consciousness-body beyond, and yet permeating, time-space, the experience of which is rapture.

Here corporeality is understood differently than physicality or the experience of separateness. Divine corporeality is unity and simplicity, and the "persons" of the Trinity are experienced not as separate beings, but as divine aspects within the globe of eternity. The experience of the globe of eternity is likened to an eye that sees itself, that is, to the experience of divine self-consciousness. There is no divine anger within the globe of eternity, because there is nothing at which to be angry, since everything within the globe is the divine corporeal-eternal self-consciousness. In the inward court of the divine are what Pordage terms "simplified spirits," which are the profoundly simple and unified divine ministering spirits that act as divine executors or ministers and yet themselves are aspects of divine consciousness of the divine. A profoundly simple and unified corporeality is necessary for this divine self-consciousness within eternity.

The globe of eternity is, as the name itself implies, beyond and prior to temporo-spatiality—it refers to the nature of divine consciousness prior to the creation of eternal nature, within which the visible or four-elementary material world exists. One can understand this metaphysics as akin to a series of concentric spheres. 'Outside' and permeating the spheres is the transcendent Nothing, the divine atmosphere. Within this divine atmosphere, the globe of eternity, the drama of temporo-spatial creation takes place within the sphere of eternal nature. Within this larger sphere, there are smaller distinct spheres, among them the angelical or heavenly-love sphere, the light-fire-world or paradisal sphere, the dark-fire or wrathful hell-sphere, and the four-elemental sphere of visible nature.

The point here is that from the perspective of John Pordage's visionary Christian theosophic metaphysics, the physical world is in fact only one comparatively small part of a much larger set of worlds or spheres, all of which exist within the realm of what he terms eternal nature, beyond which is the *Unground*, which in turn emerges out of the Nothing (German: *Nichts*). All of the smaller worlds or spheres in eternal nature, including the four-elementary, exist in an unfallen or transcendent state as the manifestation of perpetual divine self-revelation. What we customarily or ordinarily think of as the corporeal world or corporeal nature is in fact merely a fallen or divided aspect of what, originally, was the pristine, primordial corporeality that can be experienced by one who is rapt in contemplation and who enters into a particular visionary state.

Conventional accounts of Western history emphasize the progressive emergence of science and technicism, that is, of the discovery of the laws or dimensions of time-space that make possible the industrial exploitation of the world, based on concepts like gravity, energy, relativity, and so forth. Figures like Jacob Böhme or John Pordage do not figure at all in such accounts—indeed, seen in relation to the progressive development of techno-scientism, Böhme and Pordage are entirely marginal and indeed, are to be dismissed out of hand. But what if, at the inception of modernity in the seventeenth century, we now can recognize an entirely different and far more complex and profound metaphysics represented in the works of Böhme and Pordage?

If we recognize and accept the existence of this much larger gnostic cartography in the work of Böhme and Pordage, then the conventional history of what we colloquially term "modernity" is revealed as a narrowing of focus to merely the manipulable and exploitable physical world. What before was seen or depicted as inexorable progress might, from this different and wider perspective be revealed as regress or deviation away from the larger metaphysical context, without which the individual human being appears to be cast adrift in a meaningless world, or at best merely offered the possibility of "creating one's own meaning," one set of values being then just as good as another. This, of course, describes the existential situation characterizing most of Western/modern humanity during the twentieth century, and certainly defining figures like Sartre, or Camus, or even Picasso, Rauschenberg, and many others.

What I am suggesting here, in other words, is that to understand what happened over the course of "modernity," that is, to Western civilization from the seventeenth to the twenty-first centuries, we might well need to understand an alternative metaphysics that *also* existed at the beginning of Western "modernity." This alternative metaphysics, represented by Böhme and Pordage, is very similar to the Plotinian and Gnostic currents of late antiquity, and just as those visionary traditions (whose exemplars certainly pointed beyond the horizon of history) were shunted aside by a prevailing historicist current (one enforced during the medieval period by the Inquisitional apparatus), so too in early modernity we find that the same kind of war was waged once again, and once again the prevailing narrative was the most reductive one, the one that rejected, excluded, and derided such gnostic figures as Böhme and Pordage who could have formed the foundation of a more profound and balanced worldview.

We see aspects of such a worldview in other esoteric traditions of the early modern period, such as alchemy, but alchemical or magical traditions are by their very nature closer to the physical sciences and to historicity than is the metaphysics of a Böhme or a Pordage. Only in the works of these figures, and in Jewish Kabbalah, do we see a complete metaphysics that includes not only a cartography of hidden spheres (cosmological realms and principles/eternal nature/sephira) but also a metaphysics centered on transcendence (Unground/Nichts/Keter/Ain soph). Both Jewish and Christian mysticism existed at the inception of modernity as complete alternative philosophico-religious perspectives, and both were stones that the builders of modernity necessarily rejected.

Industrial-technical modernity emerged from the rejection of a more profound cosmology and metaphysics—indeed, such a rejection is in part a precondition for and in part a symptom of the emergence of secularity. After all, the rejection of a more complete gnostic cosmology and metaphysics was built into Christianity from very early on, and from well before Augustine was already deeply entrenched in the West. This rejection was a precondition for the emergence of secularity because confessional Christianity long since had rejected what is beyond the horizon of history, and had mostly pushed aside even an Eckhart and a Tauler who had pointed toward the rejected stone. But the advent of Protestantism, and almost immediately thereafter, of modern secularity, was really the culmination of this rejection. What Christianity had begun with its early rejection of gnostic figures, outright secularity eventually completed in its rejection of religion as a whole.

What becomes clear from the work of a Böhme or a Pordage is that what lies beyond the horizon of history is nonetheless not "elsewhere," or even (in any ultimate sense) "beyond," but in fact present and directly accessible to us. Beyond the horizon of history are the dynamic principles that inform existence here and now. These dynamic principles are accessible because they are both in the cosmos and in us—indeed, they are within and yet beyond us, that is, they are not identifiable with us as individuals. We see very much the same kind of perspectives in Hinduism and in Buddhism, the religions that are closest to the experiential Christian gnostic tradition of Böhme and Pordage. Advaita Vedanta and Mahayana Buddhism both emphasize the nondual transcendence at the heart of existence, which we see reflected in the works of, most notably for our purposes, the modern Japanese philosopher Keiji Nishitani.[65]

Nishitani, in a seminal discussion entitled "Shunyata and History," discusses at length the Jewish and Christian predilection for linear history, messianism, and apocalyptic millennialism. His critique of Western historicism emerges from Zen Buddhism, and more broadly from the Mahayana Buddhist *sutra* tradition as represented in works like the *King of Samadhi Sutra*. Although this critique may seem to be from an entirely different perspective than mine, in fact it is profoundly akin to and confirms what we have seen here. Nishitani writes that historical time as it emerged in Judaism and Christianity, dependent on the notion of historical beginning and ending points generated by a somehow personal or tribal God, is in fact a kind of "optical illusion" or to put it another way, a fiction.[66] This notion of historical time as linear is, of course, shared by secular historicism, which substitutes "progress" or "evolution" for a divine engine, but in either case, history is drawn toward a *telos* or an *eschaton*. From a Buddhist perspective, for a whole variety of reasons, such a perspective is simply mistaken, and Nishitani makes this quite clear.

But what is the alternative? Nishitani locates the answer in the Buddhist concept (and experience) of *shunyata*, or transcendence, which of course has a Western counterpart in Böhme's and Pordage's concept (and experience) of the *Nichts*, or Nothing out of which the *Ungrund* or Unground perpetually emerges. *Shunyata* or *Nichts* can be described as the timeless or eternal present out of which time ceaselessly emerges. Nishitani describes *shunyata* as an openness at the bottom of the present or of existence, a kind of bottomlessness. Pordage likewise describes his experience of the *Ungrund* when he ceased to look elsewhere or outward, and instead his consciousness relaxed, and sank at rest into the Unground.[67]

This is significant: there is here a deep meeting of East and West, which emerges from the direct experientiality of gnosis in Mahayana Buddhism and in Christian theosophic mysticism. Philosophically, or metaphysically, these two perspectives are profoundly similar, and we see this in their implied critique of both Judeo-Christian and secular historicism. In Nishitani's work, the West is critiqued from a perspective culturally and religiously external, whereas what we see in Pordage is that the potential for exactly the same kind of critique was present *in the West itself at the seventeenth-century beginning of "modernity."* What is more, from the affirmative side, a Christian metaphysics profoundly analogous to Buddhist metaphysics was also present at the inception of "modernity."

But we should be clear. The critique of linear historicism is not a rejection of history, nor does it reflect an effort to "escape" from history, as someone like Eric Voegelin wrongly claimed of ancient Gnostics and of anyone whose politics he or his acolytes didn't like. It is, rather, a recognition that linear historicism is a kind of optical illusion—it seems the only true or authentic perspective only because it rests upon the rejecting or ignoring of the gnostic metaphysics of a Pordage. Pordage, like Nishitani, did not seek to "escape" or reject history, but instead recognized that there are different kinds of time, what we could call degrees of time, just as there are kinds or degrees of materiality. Of these, physicality and linear temporality are only the coarsest.

Pordage's writing makes clear that there are intermediate realms between us and absolute transcendence—indeed, many of his works, like *Göttliche und Wahre Metaphysica*—are detailed explorations of such realms. Dwellers in those intermediate realms include angels and simplified spirits, who exist in eternities, that is, in kinds of time or duration unfathomable in relation to our own familiar and fleeting temporality. The Gnostics of antiquity like Valentinus referred to aeons, and Buddhism refers to *kalpas*, but in any case Pordage clearly refers to eternity and to a kind of purified or refined light-materiality that corresponds to what we might term eternal time. There are, in other words, different kinds of metaphysical existence, and different kinds of eternity depending upon one's sphere within eternal nature.

Eternal nature exists, Pordage tells us, for the purpose of divine self-revelation. It is the medium through which we can ascend toward the divine, or toward the divine self-awareness, and it is simultaneously the necessary medium through which the divine can descend or reveal itself in luminosity. One thinks here of Einsteinian physics, that is, of metaphysical dimensions of light, matter, and energy. In eternal nature—not fallen eternal nature, its distorted reflection, but in the pristine original unity—light as divine self-awareness penetrates and manifests itself to itself as material luminosity, or light-matter in eternity.

Different degrees of eternity correspond to kinds of consciousness, which in turn correspond to different forms of materiality. At the most rarefied dimensions, consciousness is not even an appropriate word anymore, because it implies at least some subtle degree of duality. By contrast, Pordage writes, in the realm of the simplified spirits within still eternity, although the spirits are distinct, they are more like sparks of light or divine eyes, for they share thoughts, see through one eye, hear through one ear, speak with one voice, and share a single body.[68] Beyond this unity is the unfathomable unity of the Trinity, which is akin to an eye that sees itself, that is, to unfathomable divine self-awareness and loving delight.

At this point, we can see the comparative absurdity of those polemicists who, as I discussed in detail in *The New Inquisitions*, see what they construe as "Gnostics" as particularly frightening because "Gnostics" are those who seek to "escape" or to "reject" history. What we see rather in Pordage is more like an adventurer in the realms beyond the physical, and beyond what we customarily think of as time. In his writings, we discover that his adventures reveal not an imagined bogeyman, but rather such alarming dimensions or aspects of the divine as eternity, love, and rapture. Beyond the horizon of history is not a frightening specter, but ascending degrees of progressively more unified and transcendent divine self-awareness, culminating in what cannot be conveyed in words at all.

What might the political implications be of this ecstatic ascent into the inexpressible? That is the subject of our next chapter.

Chapter Eight

Negative Theology and Politics

The modern era could be construed as the era of rights—or to put it another way, of affirmative freedom. The right to private property, the right to vote, the right of a prisoner of war to be treated humanely, these were hard-fought rights, often being asserted only after a bloody war, as the vote after the American Civil War, or the Geneva Conventions after World War II. What we think of as rights indeed are often affirmative rights, that is, freedom *to*, as in freedom to move about freely, freedom to vote, freedom to buy and sell as one pleases, freedom to speak one's mind publicly, and so forth. These liberties to do this or that are in fact precious—they are arguably the single greatest intellectual achievement of the modern era. But it is easily, too easily forgotten that the foundation of civil liberties, or affirmative freedom, is negative freedom. And as we will see, negative freedom in turn is most profoundly understood only in relation to negative theology.

The widespread, if by no means universal affirmation of civil liberties and human rights is an admirable, aspirational response to the nightmares of the nineteenth and twentieth centuries, which manifested mostly in the form of horrific wars. It is worth observing again that the widespread assertion of the Geneva Conventions after the conflagrations of World War II is one of the signal human achievements of the twentieth century. Of course the Convention against torture did not eliminate it, but it created the standard by which civilization could be recognized and affirmed against tyrannical barbarism. A nation-state by virtue of the Conventions knew that its conduct could be judged against that standard, and when successive United States presidential administrations sought to flout or circumvent the Conventions in the first decade of the twenty-first century, they could only do so by attempting to weasel around them: the Conventions stand as a clear indication of what aspirational civilization means, and of what kind of conduct is outlawed by virtue of being civilized.

But affirmative rights, including the right to hold property and the rights to life and liberty, rest ultimately on a foundation of negative freedom, that is, on a foundation of *freedom-from*. Of course this concept has historical significance. The greatest achievements of Western civilization in developing Anglo-European-American jurisprudence are instances of negative freedom, as in the case of *habeus corpus*, that is, the right of citizens *not* to be imprisoned at the whim of a monarch. One must know the charges against one; one must be subject to a legal process. The right to a trial by a jury of one's peers, the right to know the charges against one, the right to legal representation in a court of law—all of these affirmative rights are in fact means of enforcing negative freedom. These ideas entail a freedom from tyrannical caprice.

But I would argue that, great as are the historical significances of these juridical achievements, they rest upon a profound, if almost totally unrecognized theological foundation. Much of popular Christian theology is affirmative; it is built around the comforting notion of a personal God, a Father-deity who looks over and intervenes in human affairs. Here we are not considering theological subtleties so much as the broader array of popular perspectives that can be found in Protestantism and in Roman Catholicism as well as in Eastern Orthodoxy. All of these Christian traditions in turn are indebted to the Jewish notion of a tribal God, a jealous, partial, often wrathful God that we see in the Old Testament and that keeps recurring in fundamentalist or what I would term externalist forms of Christianity, Judaism, and Islam.

The notion of a personal or a tribal God reflects a deeply embedded I-thou relationship—it offers a relational personal identity to the believer. This new or reinforced personal identity in turn often creates a sense of the individual as somehow deputized to speak for the personal God whom he represents. Thus we see the emergence of orthodoxy as opposed to "heresy," of the "righteous (or self-righteous) believers" who believe that it is in the best interest of others that they enforce their own beliefs. And thus, too, we see eventually the emergence of the Inquisition, that is, of doctrinal constructions that seem to the righteous believers to require enforcement even by bloodletting and torture. "Our" God supports "our war" against "the heathen."

State or political fundamentalism and inquisitionalism has the same underlying origin and dynamic as does its religious forebears—that is, all of them derive from the identification of the "I" with a politico-religious ideology that offers a deceptive self-identity. "I" am validated by virtue of the ideology or the doctrines, and the more that the "I" enforces that ideological vision upon others in order to create an imagined future utopia, the more that apparent identity is reinforced in contrast to the "not-I," that is, to the unbelievers, the "heretics," or the dissidents. The "I" can puff itself up when it makes itself into a True Believer, for now it has assumed a new identity. But this identity, one must remember, is from the outside—it is *exoteric.*

If fundamentalism or inquisitionalism are the extreme results of personalist theology, they are matched to some extent by a parallel movement in affirmative political rights, which as it grows more distorted, become a set of demands (as in identity politics), and in the most extreme forms become a set of ideological doctrines that must be enforced by bloody means upon the people. Both of these theological and political trajectories quickly become grotesque as they are applied, and produce totalizing centralized bureaucratic apparatuses that in turn claim victims in the name of their respective religious or secular doctrines. In both cases, "I" discover "my identity" by serving my personal God (which may be the state) through compelling and coercing others.

Typically, this coercion turns into violence, into the strange notion that if one were to persecute or kill others, such actions would bring about an apocalyptic millennium. Violent attempts at coercion are the sure sign that the ideocratic "I" has hardened completely against the "heretical" other who will not submit, or who is imagined to be the religio-political enemy. And so the essential dualism of the religio-political is revealed—the "I" takes on its full false identity by imprisoning, torturing, or killing the politico-religious "not-I." Whether it is a "secular" state or a religious institution, whether it is identified with a tribal god or with a set of ideological doctrines is not so important as the activation of this dualistic pathology that cries for victims.

There are checks, of course, both politically and theologically, on such behavior. Politically, the check is negative freedom—that is, the kinds of freedoms from centralized authority that are built into the American Bill of Rights, that place checks on the powers of the centralized state and its bullying bureaucracies. Theologically, the check is negative theology—that is, theology that refuses the simplistic assertions of theistic personalism

91

or tribalism, and instead insists upon the indescribability and the sheer transcendence of the Divine. Such a Divine is pure presence, and there is no "I" to be puffed up by it.

Whereas politico-religious fundamentalisms are inherently exoteric, negative theology is inherently esoteric. That is, negative theology points not toward some exoteric enforcement upon others, but toward the esoteric, that is, toward inner verification for oneself of sheer transcendence. Thus we should not be surprised that in modernity, which is relentlessly exoterizing in every direction, we do not find much hint that the esoteric or that negative theology ever even existed, let alone that it might exist in the midst of modernity itself. Where are the negative theologians, where are the mystics who belong to the tradition of Dionysius the Areopagite, of Eckhart, of the Divine Darkness? We look for them in modernity, but in vain. Why is that?

Exoterism is based on obedience, on a set of external requirements or demands, codified into laws. The modern Western "secular" states in fact mimic this monotheistic exoterism, and this is true for all forms of political correctness, whether communist, fascist, or managerial. In all modern states, the managerial state becomes the enforcer of political theology, that is, of commandments that are held to result from political covenants, observance of which is imagined to lead "the people" to the promised land, to an earthly paradise, and so forth.

Negative theology, because it is inherently esoteric, is in the West mostly in a polar relationship with exoteric monotheism. Whereas exoterism is externalist and based on obedience to proscriptions—exactly what we see transposed from religious traditions into secular modern society, where central governments have codified requirements for all manner of personal behavior, and intruded into every aspect of one's life and personal freedom—esoterism is internally oriented and as a result its practitioners are not interested in monitoring or controlling the lives or details of the lives of other people.

Of course, as soon as one begins to use terms like "gnosis" or even to refer to negative theology, this will make the devotees of exoterism nervous. For some reason, in the West, those inclined toward exoterism have tended to regard esoterism with suspicion, and even to claim that those who seek the "secret roads inward" are somehow dangerous, or destructive to "social order." Why this might be, of course, they never can make clear, no doubt because it is not true. The exoteric opposition to esoterism derives, not from anything intrinsic to esoterism, but rather from the fundamental difference in perspective and disposition between the two: one looks outward, toward others; the other looks inward.

Yet the inward turn of the gnostic or mystic has political implications. Its central implication is libertarian. Someone who turns inward is, more or less by definition, not interested in power, in controlling others, in constructing authoritarian or totalitarian social systems. The essential social problem resulting from the inward turn: that it effectively strengthens the position of the exoterist because the contemplative has turned away from the managerial state. In other words, the primary objection to encouraging the inward turn is that turning away from the affairs of state only gives power to those who do not so turn away, but instead seek it, often for the worst reasons.

However, one also has to ask to what extent this objection would hold in the kind of state that we are envisioning here: a non-centralized or distributed, agrarian and craft culture that includes a place of honor for the contemplative life. Such a culture is not merely slightly different from secular modernity—it is profoundly different, and objections that indeed would hold in secular, managerial-industrial society may not be valid in the new cultures. Indeed, the essential difference is culture itself, that is, the religious orientation that pervades society and, in visible and invisible ways, orients people's lives toward communalism, altruism, and ultimately, toward contemplative realization.

The new cultures we are envisioning here are, of course, not entirely new, because they have their antecedents and roots in the West and, for that matter, in Asia as well. Those roots are twofold: politically, in negative freedom, and theologically, in the *via negativa*. Both of these represent checks, politically, on the centralized state's assertion of power, and theologically, on the centralized church's assertions about the nature of the personalized tribal divinity. Checks on government like *habeus corpus*, or the right to a fair trial, or the right to speak one's mind publically, are effectively negative freedoms since they represent freedom from the insertion of government authority into the realm of the individual. Likewise, the *via negativa* is the negation of assertions that otherwise allowed, indeed, encouraged the church to step into the realm of individual freedom in order to say that one must believe this or that doctrine or suffer the inquisitional consequences.

One of the great contributions of the West to the world is the concept of negative freedom, that is, of freedom from unjust behavior on the part of meddling authoritarians in a federal government or in a centralized church hierarchy. This idea of negative freedom, that is, freedom-from, goes very far back in the West, thousands of years, to the distributed families and tribes of Northern Europe whose successors refused to submit to the Roman imperial army and bureaucracy. The Western legacy of freedom-from or negative freedom has deep and ancient roots, much deeper than most realize.

In the same way, negative theology also has ancient roots in the West, and even though one scarcely can find any references to it, let alone exponents of it in the modern era, that fact only underscores its significance for what I am terming emergent cultures. Modern, technological society is built upon an exoteric foundation, and consists in the exclusion of negative theology and its implications, precisely because of its implications, just alluded to. But for exactly that reason, I am suggesting that negative theology is in fact the stone that had been rejected by the builders of modernity, but that represents the true keystone for emergent cultures.

Both negative freedom and negative theology will be essential for emergent cultures because they represent the refusal of politico-theological assertions of absolute human power or authority; they represent limitations on political authority and on theological authority. The word "negative" represents a sphere of possibility, an opening that allows for individual freedom and for contemplative personal verification. Those who fetishize "order" in society do not understand that authentic order is not imposed from without, but develops from within. This development only takes place when there is a space of freedom from interference in which it can happen. The indispensable guarantor of a space of freedom is the *via negativa*, both politically and theologically.

In the new cultures of the future, negative freedom will be paramount because it is so obvious what happens when negative freedom, that is, freedom from the power of the centralized state, is curtailed. Managerial bureaucracy belongs to a spectrum at whose far end is totalitarianism, and most of this spectrum derives from technological thinking applied to humanity. Human beings become instrumentalized and objectified by those who represent the centralized state; the value of the human and local is obliterated in favor of the abstract, the ideological, and the national or global. The human and the local, the cultural can survive in the space created by the precious inheritance of the West, the tradition of negative freedom or freedom-from. One can foresee that fierce battles will have to be waged against centralized states at some point in order to reassert this profoundly important tradition of the West, to create space for emergent cultures.

Even more important than negative political freedom, though, is negative theological freedom. At first glance, of course, negative political freedom would seem to be more important. And of course it is vital for a living culture. But essential, as we will shortly see, is a cultural center or origin and font. This cultural font is non-dualistic, transcendent, beyond description, let alone objectification and control. It is the transcendent origin of culture; it is what culture points toward and what it in turn reflects. The term "negative theology" belongs to the rationalistic tradition and is itself sterile and lifeless, yet what it describes is not lifeless but the divine origin and meaning of life and of cultures.

Negative theology refers to the inexpressible heart of transcendent religious experience, not just of any kind, but of a very precise kind. The great Neoplatonic philosopher Plotinus recognized this when in *Enneads* he describes the Good, the Being beyond that "neither strives, since it feels no lack, nor attains, since it has no striving." It is "in need of nothing, and therefore possesses nothing beyond itself."[69] To speak of it or to apply terms to it is only to add deficiency to it because it is not itself an object or subject to objectifying thinking. As a result, it also is not subject to institutionalization or to the construction of dogmatic certitudes, because it is itself the experience of good and of union as awareness, but awareness only of what it is as plenitude.

This is a critically important point. Negative theology is prior to political negative freedom because negative theology is the refusal of dogmatic certitudes that take on doctrinal force and become the substructure around which the exoteric institution is generated. In Christianity, this exoteric institutionalism is commonly more strictly religious, but in Islam one finds the theopolitical more often, the most extreme form of which is the exoteric theopolitical state ruled by mullahs or clerisy, or by what we might term a clerified laity, as in the case of the Taliban. In all cases, though, one finds the generation of dogmatic certitudes on the basis of which people seek to persecute or to kill others. Negative theology shatters such certitudes because it reveals what transcends them; it is the revelation of what transcends language, through language.

It is no accident that one finds so few modern exemplars of this negative theological tradition that stretches back all the way to antiquity, not only to Basilides, of course, but to the Platonic and Gnostic traditions. Nor is it any accident that Basilides was not incorporated into what became confessional institutionalized Christianity; and indeed, even Dionysius the Areopagite was only partly allowed in. Across the theological

95

spectrum in modern Christianity, one looks long and hard to find even a trace of negative theology. Why is that? It is because Christianity gave birth to secular technological society, and exists within it, sharing the same underlying dualism, the same basic attitudes toward humanity as separate from nature, the same historocentrism, and the same rejection of the esoteric and of negative theology.

It is not that negative theology is rejected consciously, that is, persecuted in orthodoxy or in secular modernity—rather, it is that negative theology represents a fundamentally different mode of consciousness, one entirely foreign to exoteric Christianity or to its bastard children, secular technological societies. This other mode of consciousness is fundamentally free in ways that conventional theology cannot be; it is not that it feels free to do whatever it likes, but rather that it is no longer captured by this or that objectifying tendency, no longer attaching to and reifying this or that projection of tribal identity or deity as absolute and as somehow honored by atrocities like the sacrifice of others. Negative theology represents the transcendence of objectifying consciousness.

We can go further, because negative theology points toward what Nicholas Berdyaev called the "meontic," that is, toward the transcendence of the ontic, of the realm of being and becoming. This meontic center is actually the origin-point of cultures; it is the juncture of this-worldly and transcendent consciousness out of which culture and meaning ceaselessly are born. Negative theology has been excluded for the most part from contemporary theology, but its very absence is a kind of presence, indeed, the keystone essential for the emergence of new cultures and, eventually, for the accompanying new polis whose hallmark will be the negative freedom that is the enduring legacy of what is represented theologically as the negative way.

Chapter Nine

Modernity and the Secret Roads Inward

Understanding intellectual lineages is vital if we are to understand our own era more clearly and deeply. It is not enough to investigate this or that figure in isolation. An author who is worth reading has many forebears, so by recognizing them, one comes to understand not only the work of a given individual but also much larger currents that have shaped and that continue to shape the often hidden intellectual architecture of our time. In what follows, we will disentangle and tease out from the skein two primary hidden lines shaping the substructure or intellectual infrastructure of "secular modernity."

The first of these lines is Thomas Hobbes, carried on into the twentieth century by those who speak for authoritarianism like Carl Schmitt. I have written elsewhere about Schmitt and his anti-mysticism, so here I will limit my remarks. Schmitt's well-known friend/foe distinction reflects the orthodox/heretic dynamic built into early Christianity by Tertullian and other definitive figures of late antiquity. For Tertullian, as for Schmitt, historicity has absolute precedence over the docetic view that Christ did not come in the flesh but belongs to another world. Tertullian bitterly attacks those he deems heretics, venomously likening them to scorpions. Echoing this, in an aside in "The Visibility of the Church," Schmitt remarks "every religious sect which has transposed the concept of the Church from the visible community of believing Christians into a *corpus mere mysticum* basically has doubts about the humanity of the Son of God. It has falsified the historical reality of the incarnation of Christ into a mystical and imaginary process."[70] For Schmitt, too, mysticism is congruent with docetism; it is "imaginary;" mysticism is false because, he imagines, it has "falsified" history.

97

It becomes clearer, then, why Schmitt endorsed Tertullian as the prototypical political theologian. Both Tertullian and Schmitt insist on the primacy of the historical. In *Nomos of the Earth*, Schmitt proposes the *historical* importance within Christianity of the concept of the *katechon*, or "restrainer" that creates the possibility of Christian empire, brought about by "the historical power to *restrain* the appearance of the Antichrist and the end of the present eon."[71] The notion of a *katechon* is taken from an obscure Pauline verse, II Thessalonians 2.6-7: "And you know what is restraining him now so that he may be revealed in his time. For the mystery of lawlessness is already at work; only he who now restrains it will do so until he is out of the way." The *katechon* represents, for Schmitt, an "historical concept" of "potent historical power" that preserves the "tremendous historical monolith" of a Christian empire, and it does so by opposing the perceived activity of Satan in others.[72] One can hardly avoid the paramount importance of historicity here.

Schmitt is a political and geopolitical theorist whose political theology represents an insistence upon antagonism and combat as the foundation of politics, reflecting Tertullian's emphasis on antagonism toward heretics as the foundation of theology. A confirmed dualist, Tertullian even wanted to continue his orthodox/heretic [friend/enemy] dynamic into the afterlife, asserting that "There will need to be carried on in heaven persecution [of Christians] even, which is the occasion of confession or denial."[73] Likewise, Schmitt writes, in *The Concept of the Political*, that "a theologian ceases to be a theologian when he . . . no longer distinguishes between the chosen and the nonchosen."[74] When he writes "the high points of politics are simultaneously the moments in which the enemy is, in concrete clarity, recognized as the enemy," the theological antecedent of this statement is that, from Tertullian's perspective, the high point of theology is the recognition of "heretics" or of "heresy."[75] Schmitt insists on "the fundamental theological dogma of the evilness of the world and man" and rejects those who deny original sin, i.e., "numerous sects, heretics, romantics, and anarchists."[76]

Schmitt was only one of many who, in the twentieth century, derived their political theory from the work of Thomas Hobbes, whose somewhat pessimistic views emerged in part as a response to the chaos of the English civil war era, but also in the historical context of what can only be termed a remarkable efflorescence of esotericism not seen since late antiquity. Hobbes's *Leviathan* arguably signals an intellectual origin-point of the modern secular state, and it is little surprise that Schmitt devoted considerable space to Hobbes in his 1938 *The Leviathan in the State Theory of Thomas Hobbes*. Schmitt accepted the Hobbesian emphasis on the authority of the sovereign, and the Hobbesian belief in original sin was congenial too. But Schmitt also recognized the larger esoteric context in which Hobbes emerged—that is, that the early modern period represented what can best be described as an esoteric renaissance.[77]

Revealingly, in his discussion of Hobbes Schmitt cites the influential French esoteric author René Guénon's *La Crise du monde moderne* (1927), and specifically Guénon's observation that the collapse of medieval civilization into early modernity by the seventeenth century came about because of secret forces operating in the background.[78] Guénon saw the early modern period as inaugurating the progressive decline that modernity represents for him, which would conclude in the appearance of the Antichrist and the end of the world. For him, as for Schmitt, individualistic Protestantism entailed deterioration from prior medieval unity, and accordingly in *Leviathan*, Schmitt is especially critical of "secret societies and secret orders, Rosicrucians, freemasons, illuminates, mystics and pietists, all kinds of sectarians, the many 'silent ones in the land,' and above all, the restless spirit of the Jew who knew how to exploit the situation best until the relation of public and private, deportment and disposition was turned upside down."[79]

Like Hobbes's, Schmitt's perspective is implicitly critical of the subjectification and inward or contemplative turn characteristic of those who travel "the secret road" "that leads inward." Romantics, mystics, Jews, Schmitt holds, "as differently constituted as were the Masonic lodges, conventicles, synagogues, and literary circles, as far as their political attitudes were concerned, they all displayed by the eighteenth century their enmity toward the leviathan elevated to a symbol of state."[80] Esoteric groups and individual figures, like Romantic poets, represented an inward turn that was also skeptical and perhaps even hostile to centralized state power.

Like Hobbes, Schmitt is pessimistic about the human condition. The leviathan symbolizes the awful but, in his view, necessary power of the centralized state, necessary because it can restrain or postpone the larger decline that modernity represents. Man is inclined toward evil by nature and must be controlled by an outside force (the centralized state). In *Leviathan*, Schmitt deplores the split between inner and outer life represented by esoteric groups and individuals, and by the subjectification represented by Romanticism during the early modern period. Those who represent the "inward turn" are viewed as that which the *katechon* restrains; they represent fragmentation and decline. To restrain such fragmentation was the task enjoined by Juan Donoso Cortés in his defense of the Inquisition, and by Dostoevsky's Grand Inquisitor in *The Brothers Karamazov*.[81]

It is interesting to consider Schmitt's later (1949) linking of Hobbesian statist philosophy with none other than "the domestication of Christ undertaken by Dostoyevsky's Grand Inquisitor." For, Schmitt continues, "Hobbes gave voice to and provided a scientific reason for what the Grand Inquisitor is–to make Christ's impact harmless in the social and political spheres, to dispel the anarchistic nature of Christianity while leaving it a certain legitimating effect, if only in the background."[82] Of course, it is a charmingly perverse interpretation of Dostoevsky's great character, the Grand Inquisitor, to assert that his purpose was to "make Christ's impact harmless in the social and political spheres." Dostoevsky's novel reveals something rather different about the Grand Inquisitor, and "harmless" doesn't quite describe it.

Hobbes's work functions very well as a predecessor to twentieth-century state totalism, and this is exactly why someone like Schmitt was so attracted to him. Further, this is also why many Leftist or "Leftist" intellectuals of the late twentieth century laid some emphasis on Schmitt: his work represents defense of authoritarianism and a sustained attack on parliamentary democratism or republicanism that many post-communist, post-Marxist intellectuals found useful even if its National Socialist ambience is more than a little unsavory.[83] Hobbes is the premier theorist of centralized state power, and his approach is appealing both to the putative Right and to the putative Left for this very reason. The late twentieth-century fashionable interest in Schmitt is an extension of this same appeal.

But there is another figure from the same period whose work remains unjustly obscure: Johannes Althusius (1557-1638). Althusius is the author of the extraordinarily erudite treatise on what today we would term "federalism," *Politica* (1603). Althusius's vision is essentially the opposite of Hobbesianism. Whereas Hobbes esteems the centralized state with an authoritarian potentate at its head, Althusius extols the people and a decentralized vision. Although he was a Calvinist, Althusius's decentralist emphasis is very close to the later Roman Catholic notion of "subsidiarity," that is, the view that political authority belongs to the people and their communities first, and that any other authority derives from that originary power. Thus, whatever can be handled by a family or a community, should be handled by them. The only purpose of the larger state is to provide what cannot be provided otherwise, like collective military protection.

Whereas Hobbes believed that the centralized state (leviathan) and the sovereign are central to the polis, Althusius argued that the polis developed organically, and even used the term "symbiotics" to describe the way his decentralized state functions. Politics, for Althusius, is "the art of associated men for the purpose of establishing, culvitating, and conserving social life among them." When people draw together, they form an association based on their common interests. His vision of the polis is thus indebted to the medieval guilds and cooperatives, that is, *collegia* united through the holy vocation of voluntary association. A ruler is thus more of a solon, a member of an elder group (termed *ephors*) of those whose judgment is trusted by the community.

A realm only exists as a confederation of cities, provinces, or regions, and it is held together only by mutual trust informed by common aims and ideals. A ruler is one who administers such a realm, and his authority is not beyond civil law. Rather, the ruler is also limited by natural and divine law, and if a fair civil law is enacted by a ruler, then how could he be exempt from it? If the ruler is exempt, Althusius reasons, then he exemplifies unfairness. Furthermore, Althusius continues, the king or ruler has no authority on his own, only the authority granted him by the people and communities. A sovereign does not have supreme power above the law, nor is sovereignty his personal property.[84]

Thus we can see that Althusius offers us an important alternative to the Hobbesian model. The Hobbesian polis is based not on cooperation but on fear; its authority rests on the dualism of either/or, friend/enemy. In this respect, it derives from the Old Testament model of blind fealty to the absolutely authoritative divine sovereign. By contrast, Althusius's polis is based on cooperation and mutual trust; and it rejects an authoritarian or dualistic model in favor of a confederacy derived from shared ideals. The Hobbesian polis insists upon fealty to the sovereign; the Althusian polis insists upon fealty to one's family and community, and to a confederacy only secondarily.

The Althusian polis is confederal and decentralized; its basis is individual and tribal or communal liberty and responsibility, the traditional model of the West going back to the Northern tribal confederations of millennia past. Although the Althusian model itself comes into being on the cusp of what is loosely termed "modernity," its range of citations and allusions reveal that it is not unique to Althusius, but rather is more like a compendium of political-economic learning from the time of Plato and Aristotle onward. It includes elements of both ancient pagan and later Roman Catholic traditions, condensed into a form applicable to the modern period.

What we realize, as we read Althusius, is that there are essentially two directions of Western political thought in the modern period. One, along Hobbesian lines, assumes that the individual will go astray unless the machinery of the sovereign state is there to protect him from himself, and from the nastiness of other people. This direction of Western thought leads inexorably toward the centralized bureaucratic state, and toward the constant accrual of state power over the individual. The other direction of Western thought emphasizes the responsibility and liberty of the individual within a community. It is revealing that this Althusian direction—which is also the direction of Thomas Jefferson, the Jeffersonians, and the Antifederalists of the early American period—was almost totally occluded during the later nineteenth and twentieth centuries. The Hobbesian direction, toward centralized bureaucratic power, unquestionably dominated this period, both in political praxis and in academic theory.

There were some exceptions, of course. One was Wilhelm Röpke (1899-1966), the great Swiss economist and political theorist, spokesman for decentralization and for the Swiss federalist model. Röpke's work is very much in the tradition for which Althusius also spoke—having witnessed first hand the disastrous rise of National Socialism in Germany, having spoken out against it, and having relocated to nearby Switzerland, Röpke was particularly well suited as an advocate for a decentralized, federated social and political structure with ancient Western roots. Whereas Althusius spoke on behalf of a confederal and decentralized polis at the inception of modernity, Röpke did so in the twentieth century, in full view of what monstrosities were spawned by modern mass society in a centralized, authoritarian polis.

Here, then, are the parallel figures: Hobbes and Althusius on the brink of the seventeenth century, Schmitt and Röpke in the midst of the twentieth.

* * *

Far from belonging only to a mostly-forgotten and distant era of late antiquity, questions concerning "heresy" and "orthodoxy," "gnosis" and "anti-gnosis" are of great importance if we are to more clearly understand what we may call the intellectual substructure of our own time. Here I am not referring only to what we may call the "secularization hypothesis," meaning the view that modernity emerged from the secularization of Christian theology and culture. Such a perspective is certainly visible in the work of Max Weber on Protestantism and capitalism, as also in the work of Carl Schmitt on what he termed "political theology," which is more allied to Roman Catholicism. There is much to be said for the "secularization hypothesis" as a way of interpreting why and how secular modernity came into existence.

Understanding the origins of secular modernity, and in particular understanding the emergence of secular modernity's most concentrated form—totalitarianism—requires understanding the history of Christianity, going all the way back to late antiquity and the formation of Christian "orthodoxy." Such connections have been recognized before—one thinks here of the work of Eric Voegelin or Hans Blumenberg, for instance, who posited modernity as a renewed battle of the "orthodox" against the dreaded "Gnostics."[85] Voegelin and Blumenberg were entirely misguided in their emphases, but they did recognize that there is a profound connection between modernity and the struggle in late antiquity between the "orthodox" and the "Gnostics." Where they went wrong was to uncritically accept the anti-gnostic rhetoric of late antiquity—thus, effectively, they recapitulated the heresiophobic dynamics of early "orthodox" Christianity. What they claimed was "legitimate" in modernity, or what "legitimated" modernity was what Blumenberg termed the "second overcoming of Gnosticism."[86]

Hence we are not surprised to find that Blumenberg began his *The Legitimacy of the Modern Age* by directly alluding to Voegelin's claim "the modern age 'would be better entitled the Gnostic age.'" He adds that "the old enemy who did not come from without but was ensconced at Christianity's very roots, the enemy whose dangerousness resided in the evidence that it had on its side a more consistent systematization of the biblical premises."[87] We also should not be surprised at the language here, at terms like "the old enemy," as though the "Gnostic" were synonymous with the devil himself, for this is precisely the transposed and unexamined language of heresiophobia carried over from antiquity. What is to be feared? Most of all, an "escape into transcendence."[88] Modernity is "legitimated" by an emphasis on this-worldliness, on historicity, which is also to say, on eschatology transposed into the teleology of technical/historical progress.

But when we reverse this thesis, we gain some interesting results. What if secular modernity is the logical result of the prevailing tendency in "orthodox" Western Christianity to emphasize historicity over transcendence, indeed, to anathematize as "heretical" those who insisted on transcendence of subject and object dualism? This would make secular modernity, especially in its worst, totalitarian forms, the triumph of heresiophobia. Once transcendence or gnosis is driven to the margins and excluded, then one is left only with an historical horizon. If gnosis is demonized, then there remains only the flat plain of historicity, at the far end of which hovers the specter of millennium or apocalypse. It is not far, then, once one is out on this plain, to the strictly secular millennialism of modernity as reflected in various forms of twentieth-century totalitarianism. Totalitarianism results from pursuing a distant mirage of enforced historical utopia, the pursuit of which left behind the bodies of many "heretical" victims or scapegoats.

What I am suggesting here is that "secular modernity" owes much, perhaps even almost everything, to a much earlier battle that was mostly, but never completely won in late antiquity. This is the battle against gnosis that was fought by Tertullian, Irenaeus, Epiphanius, and some others among the Ante-Nicene fathers, but a battle in which even some of their own number, notably Clement of Alexandria, took the other side and defended the value of an orthodox gnosis. A certain ambivalence remained in Western Christianity, emblematized in the works of such figures as Dionysius the Areopagite under whose auspices there remained at least some room for mysticism within the tradition. It was only in the emergence of "secular modernity" that the battle against gnosis was won again, a bit more thoroughly this time.

It is true that on the cusp of modernity, Protestantism gave birth to its greatest mystic, the inexhaustible Jacob Böhme, who died in 1624. But Böhmean theosophy, which sought to restore to Christianity its metaphysical mooring, did not establish dominance or even much of a foothold or influence in the universities or in any established churches. Indeed, Böhmean theosophy is strikingly anti-sectarian.[89] By the nineteenth century, "secular modernity" had taken hold thoroughly enough that we can hardly think of a single great mystic during the nineteenth and twentieth centuries. I discuss this problem in my historical survey *Magic and Mysticism,* and note a few major exceptions, among them Franklin Merrell-Wolff in the mid-twentieth century, who was inspired by Vedanta, and Bernadette Roberts, a Roman Catholic gnostic of the late twentieth century. But the exceptions prove the rule: who has heard of them? Even specialists in the recent history of religion overlook them.

My point here is this: "secular modernity" in the West emerged out of an even more complete banishing of gnosis than that which took place in late antiquity. What we term "secular modernity"—with all its technological prowess, its extraordinary capacity to mobilize people and machinery into a greater mechanism that can lay flat the entire earth [*mobilmachung*], to exploit and dominate other people and nature without qualms—derives from a fundamental schism within us, a profound dualism so deeply a part of society that we hardly even recognize that it is there. This division is between subject and object, a dualism upon which the exploitation of the world entirely depends.

To use the terms of Charles Péguy, when *mystique* is banished, that is the triumph of *politique. Politique* is the political philosophy of combat and calculation that remains completely engrossed in the historical and that rejects out of hand those who are drawn to the secret roads inward. *Politique* has religious antecedents, no doubt. But it is not, and cannot be religious except in the sense of affirming and defending a religion devoid of mysticism, that is, devoid of inwardness and transposed into a language of empire that unfolds in history.

And there is an interesting parallel here with the emergence of Islamic fundamentalism, especially of the al-Qaeda species, because here too, one finds the assertion of an imperial and historicist religion whose millennialism is transposed into the historical notion of a grand caliphate, sometimes mingled with the notion of a coming Mahdi. For the Islamic fundamentalist, too, the world is a field of combat; an historical plain on whose distant horizon hovers the hazy mirage of an imagined utopia, if only one could impose by force one's vision on others, kill those whom one imagines to be the minions of Satan, and so forth. For the Islamic fundamentalist of this variety, Sufism, the mysticism of Islam, is to be rejected precisely because it turns one's attention inward, and away from the projected enemy, away from the dualistic world of combat.

I mention this because the various fundamentalisms, in particular those of Islam, belong to so-called secular modernity too. They belong as much as "secular modernity," and perhaps even more, to the realm of *politique.* At least "secular modernity" has a libertarian ethos built into it, the concepts of civil liberties, of individual freedom. But the bastard children of "secular modernity," the various fundamentalisms, they are not so welcoming of those who disagree with them, of the rights of others. In truth this because they have turned even more than "secular moderns" have against the very notion of gnosis, that is, of inwardness; for them, what matters above all is indeed exactly what Schmitt recognized, the need for the "enemy," for the projected "other" who is hardened into a mere target, who is to be annihilated. Reacting against the alienation endemic to "secular modernity," they choose as a remedy an even more intense and total alienation. They are the avenging shade of "secular modernity" itself.

What then has *mystique* to offer us? Of what value are these "secret roads" inward? (I write "roads" because, given the numerous forms of esoterism, there is not only one road inward.) Let us look back at the early modern period that Guénon and Schmitt rightly recognized to be so pivotal. There was at that time, in the seventeenth and eighteenth centuries, an efflorescence of esoteric movements, notably that of alchemy, but also astrology, Christian theosophy, various other movements like Rosicrucianism, and what did these movements have in common? They sought bridges between self and other, between us and nature and spirit; to them belonged the desire for union or reunion with the Divine as it appears in us and in nature. Little wonder that they were rejected—they had to be rejected, if the subject-object division was accepted to the extent necessary to make possible the technical apparatus of industrial modernity. But they offered then, and still offer now, alternatives to the subject-object dualism that underlies, and makes possible, the condition of "secular modernity."

Indeed, one can go further. It may well be that "secular modernity" taken as a whole, recognizing both its positive and negative dimensions, nonetheless derives from and exemplifies a fundamental alienation of self and other. It is possible that the one thing needful, the rejected keystone, cannot be found in any external, technical solution, nor does it belong to the endless concatenation of dualistic combat, but rather belongs to consciousness, more specifically to the turn inward toward what Böhme called the *mysterium.* Such a turn does not belong either to a political Right or to a political Left—it belongs, rather, to a re-orientation of a being toward realizing that which is beyond being.

As Böhme recognized, we live in a dualistic world, one in which love and wrath, friendship and hostility alternate with one another. But he also suggested, just when "modernity" was emerging, that another way of being is also possible. Such a way of being has its origin not in dualism but in non-dualism that derives from gnosis, or direct insight into what he termed the *ungrund*, or divine "not-ground." The word *ungrund* is itself a refusal of objectification—it embodies *via negativa* mysticism that goes back to Meister Eckhart, to Dionysius the Areopagite, and before him, to Basilides. Does such insight—attested to in Christianity, from late antiquity onward—have political implications? Undoubtedly it does. But the rejection of mysticism built into Christianity from early on, and if anything, intensified in modernity, created an environment highly unconducive to exploring such implications.

And so here we are. The modern period has given birth to a vast array of possibilities, which is also to say, choices. It has created a space in which, for the first time in millennia, it is possible to explore openly and thoughtfully what before could not be investigated—the excluded, the suppressed, the "heretical" and esoteric currents of the past and present. Now, like in the Russian Silver Age (as John Milbank attests with his work on Sophianic Christianity), it is possible to look into the implications not just of this or that imposed political regime, but into the intellectual architecture that informs what and how we see, but that we rarely recognize or acknowledge.

The temptation is always there to recoil against the array of choices, of possibilities, to turn back toward the fixed, the comfortable, the literal, the twin familiar realms of faith and reason, even if they too often give birth to monsters. Fundamentalism is such a recoil—it is a recourse to an extreme form of dualism, seductively comforting because it provides the familiar rhetoric of believers and unbelievers, of the chosen and of the obdurate heretics. It is indeed the twin of technological-industrial rationalism, as evidenced by the technological sophistication of the jihadists with their digital video webcasts of murderous attacks, mirroring the cameras embedded in the noses of American missiles. Dualism is the foundation of modernity, as Schmitt testifies. Is it not possible, now, to begin exploring gnosis, that hidden third pillar of the West, there from antiquity, and still unspoken? Or are we rather on the brink, as the Russian Silver Age was, of descent into yet another bout of totalitarian brutalism?

Chapter Ten

"The Counter-Culture," Gnosis, and Modernity

Interpretations of the 1960s have tended to fall into two general camps. One group consists in those who trace perceived social ills back to that period, like a colleague who, morosely contemplating the failures of academe, said that one couldn't begin to rebuild the humanities and social sciences until the generation forged in that era had retired. Probably he is right, though one shouldn't be too optimistic. Another group consists in those for whom the 1960s represent the birth of a still incompleted social revolution, and for them, the era is comprehensible chiefly through Marxist interpretive lenses. The former is a pessimistic narrative of social decline and fragmentation; the latter is an optimistic narrative of partially thwarted social progress that nonetheless could be completed one day in the future. What I offer here is a very different interpretation of that era, and in particular, of the emergence of what came to be known as the "counter-culture."

Here I do not have space to discuss in detail how and where secular modernity emerged, but do have to admit the role anti-iconic Protestantism played, the Cromwellian antipathy not just to the sacred images that bore the stamp of the venerable and sacred, but also to their settings, to monasteries, statuary, and sacred sites—in short, to the indigenous cultures of the West. A similar antipathy was borne along with English and European settlers in the New World, an inherent and inextinguishable dualism of humanity and god, humanity and nature, us and them, and thus also a wake of destroyed indigenous cultures. Secular modernity, especially in North America, certainly derives from the dualism built into exoteric Judaism and Christianity.

Both communism and capitalism inherit this dualism, secularized into narratives of historical progress dependent upon the objectification of nature and of other people, which is, as Lynn White pointed out in his famous essay of 1967, in turn derived from the Jewish and Christian rejection of spirits and gods in the natural world.[90] The 1950s in many respects represent the zenith of American industrialism, and also arguably the zenith of communism—both of which are being rejected in the 1962 Port Huron Statement that called not only for a new polis, but also for a new culture. In the 1960s, something new but also ancient was being born.

Historical interpretations of the 1960s tend primarily, I would suggest, toward narratives of progress, aided by the successes of the civil rights movement in the United States during this period. In other words, the era is often interpreted as moving in a direction of social progress through history, marked and to some extent driven by social protest and conflict—by the marches against segregation and the protests against the Vietnam War, by students closing down universities or parts of them, and so forth. Such a narrative commandeers a disparate collection of events and herds them along in service to a more or less Marxist-tinged narrative of awakening socio-economic consciousness.[91] An apparently opposed narrative, obviously, is one of decline and fragmentation: from this perspective, the 1960s represent social disintegration, riots, violence, narcissistic individualism, the twilight of authority, and cultural deterioration.

But I have come to wonder about the extent to which these familiar narratives obscure our understanding of what was afoot during that era. Does a pessimistic or an optimistic narrative really help to explain what the counter-culture was? The term "counter-culture," attributed to Theodore Roszak, is very much akin to the word "antinomian," or against the nomos (community, culture). Antinomianism was a common accusation against Christian "heretics," who were said to believe themselves beyond the law, beyond conventional morality, in Nietzsche's terms, beyond good and evil. Is it possible that the counter-culture of the 1960s also represented a resurgence of archaic Western perspectives sometimes deemed "heretical"?

The late 1960s counter-culture was antinomian—often, it represented a conscious break with conventional forms of Western Christianity, and indeed, with "modernity" conceived as industrial-commercial society, and along with that, a rejection of conventional morality. Take, for instance, this excerpt from Jeff Nuttal's essay "Applications of Extasy" in the avant-garde collection *Counter Culture* (1969): "It is not very thoroughly realized in these days how completely the adherents of international culture, the culture whose surest mark is the long romantic haircut and the elaborate ornate disarray of dress, whose style is one in which the old patterns of Bohemian Europe merge with the adopted patterns of the Hindu East and the Prairie Indian, have stepped outside the morality [that] has governed civilization since the Middle Ages."[92] Strictly speaking, this is antinomianism.

I have come to think that the counterculture of the late 1960s represented a complex resurgence of what we could term the suppressed archaic, not only antinomianism, but a whole constellation of archaisms, and a conscious rejection of the conventional historical narratives of the West, both "optimistic" and "pessimistic." It also was, in a more profound sense than usually acknowledged, a rejection of secular modernity. The long hair, the fringed clothing, the communal ethos of groups like the Diggers, the widespread emergence during this period of communes, the turn toward a life lived closer to the land and to nature, all of this in retrospect may seem cliché, but taken along with intellectual statements of the period, leads me to believe that something much deeper was going on than generally is recognized.

In a 1967 statement entitled "Consciousness and Practical Action," Allen Ginsberg urged his audience "if we're going to go back to tribal wisdom, let's get back to tribal wisdom."[93] Central to Ginsberg's remarks—delivered at the Dialectics of Liberation conference convened in London by Ronald Laing, David Cooper, and Joseph Berke—is the "religious experience, the peak experience, the mystical experience, the art experience, identity experience, unitive experience of One, of all of us being one—not only ourselves [but] also one with the flowers, the very trees and plants." "Everybody's known that," Ginsberg continues, "everybody's glimpsed that and has had that natural experience."[94] He rejects "all strange forms of being," so that one treats a person as a person, not as a cop, a capitalist, a communist, a Maoist, or Allen Ginsberg, not as "self," but in a "recognition of that one which extends outward, outward, to everybody, everywhere," in short, one should embody "interpersonal Bodhisattva conduct."[95] Tibetan Buddhism plays an obvious and central role in Ginsberg's thought already at this time—he mentions Dudjom Rinpoche, a very well known Tibetan lama living in Nepal, and indeed,

Ginsberg's whole statement is an effort to, as he put it, convert San Francisco into an "electric Tibet."[96]

What makes these kinds of remarks—examples of which I can multiply at some length from other sources—important here is this: they all emphasize, in different ways, a break with the conventional narratives of Jewish and Christian historicity and dualism. We can see the break with the conventional Marxist/Communist historical narrative a few years earlier, in the Port Huron Statement, which famously calls for a New Left. It is quite clear that the authors were aware of the disastrous results of communism in the Soviet Union, and were calling for a "New Left" for just that reason—they could not believe in the historical narrative that Marxism supplied. And they did not believe in the conventional narrative of "modernity" in America supplied them from elementary school. A new vision was necessary.

In fact, a new vision is exactly what the Port Huron Statement called for. Its authors wrote, with a sense of urgency, and in words that have a particular resonance in hindsight, with our themes in mind, that "Our work is guided by the sense that we may be the last generation in the experiment with living." They wrote against the "human potentiality for violence, unreason, and submission to authority," and in favor of "self-cultivation, self-direction, self-understanding, and creativity." Their statement endorsed independence, not egotism or narcissism, but "a democracy of individual participation." They see America "without community impulse," and by implication, they seek to restore a sense of common purpose and community, but not through some grand utopian project, let alone by force. They were calling for something new.

By 1968, something new clearly had emerged, and it was not strictly or even primarily political—it was religious and cultural. That is what we see in remarks like those of Ginsberg or Nuttal or Stephen Gaskin, a charismatic figure a bit later in San Francisco. The influx of Asian religions, specifically Hinduism and Buddhism, and the rediscovery of some aspects of the West, for instance, the poetry of William Blake and through it some aspects of Western esotericism, all of these represented an infusion into "modernity" of elements that were not very easily commodifiable, that in fact represented the explicit rejection of the commodifiable, the packaged, the "modern." More than that, they represented the infusion of the vertical into the horizontal, that is, the invocation of timelessness, the assertion of the millennial present, not held off as some imagined future event as in Marxism or for that matter, in Judaism or Christianity, but as present and immediately available.

I believe that the term "counter-culture" is misleading, because it implies that there is a prevailing culture in secular modernity, and I do not think this is so.[97] Modern industrial-technical society has no culture. In fact, the *absence* of a prevailing culture is precisely what makes secular modernity so seductive—after all, industrial-technical society represents freedom from the ties of culture and indeed, of notions of sacred lands or ancestral landscapes, of the ancient gods or spirits, of ancestors and traditions, of magic and mysticism.[98] In modernity, places become homogenous, eventually interchangeable. Coming from an indigenous culture into secular modernity, suddenly one is bound not by the invisible, but only by what is visible and quantifiable. Hence the late 1960s "counter-culture" wasn't a *counter*-culture at all—since from this perspective there was no culture there to begin with—but rather was the most widespread effort since the advent of secular modernity to begin to establish culture within modernity, that is, culture in the traditional sense as reflecting and manifesting *cultus*.

It has become a commonplace to suggest that the late 1960s only could have taken place because of the extraordinary prosperity generated by mid-twentieth-century industrialism, and that is no doubt true. But what we also see quite clearly is a widespread rejection of military-industrial society, of what Lewis Mumford termed the "megamachine," and a corresponding effort to create, immediately, and not as an imagined utopia in the distant future, a living culture. One can object, of course, that the new "drop-out" culture of communes was not really a culture in the sense that it did not have a cultural center or cultural unity in the way that a traditional culture does, but rather was a pastiche of elements drawn from Hinduism, Buddhism, American Indian, and so forth. Such objections have real merit.

And yet for all that, one cannot deny that something remarkable was happening during this period, something that cannot be relegated to the negative or reactionary, that is, to simply a rejection of the military-industrial "megamachine." The 1960s and early 1970s without question generated the most widespread and affiliated communal experiments in modern history, not only in the United States, which has a history of such experiments, but also in England, Europe, indeed, around the globe. "Dropping out" referred not only to abandoning military-industrial society, but also the prevailing historicizing narratives of Judaism and Christianity, and of capitalism and communism, indeed of secular modernity, and the immediate, not indefinitely postponed creation of a new culture—not for society as a whole, but for oneself and one's family and friends.

By contrast, prevailing narratives of progress that emphasize the emergence of the Students for a Democratic Society [SDS] generally accept, as Jameson does, the notion that all of American society, or later, global modernity, must be transformed, by force if necessary, into a Marxist or quasi-Marxist ideal polis.[99] In other words, these narratives tend to accept the secular millennialism that impelled the Left through much of the nineteenth and twentieth centuries. The Weatherman phenomenon was an almost inevitable outgrowth of the secular millennialism implicit in the SDS—the Weatherman group sought to speed the coming of the millennium through violence, but both groups aimed in the same general direction, and both vaguely imagined a grandly transformed society that was nonetheless, still only a society, not a culture.[100]

What makes the communal movement born in the late 1960s so remarkable is that it rejects secular millennialist aims for society as a whole, and turns instead back toward archaic wellsprings of culture that it seeks to incarnate immediately and on a federalist, or subsidiarist model. One sees cooperation among different groups on occasion, and broader coalitions, but the center of gravity was local and immediate—the communes in many respects represented efforts to create new traditional cultures.[101] When we step back from this period and think about it in a much larger historical context, it is clear that the late 1960s represent at least in part the rebirth of the archaic in the guise of the new.

Furthermore, the underlying impetus for the "counter-culture" was not against, but rather aligned with some of the most characteristic traditions of the pre-Christian, in particular, Celtic West. These traditions were tribal and family-centered, dispersed, and organized heterarchically rather than bureaucratically/hierarchically. A heterarchy has multiple lines of authority, depending on the sphere under consideration; it is flexible, and tends more toward adventitious coalitions or confederations than toward an enduring and far-flung imperial structure like, for instance, that of Rome. In fact, we will recall the antagonism between the Celts and the Romans, as the Romans expanded their empire Westward.

In many respects, the "counter-culture" was truly pagan, pagan in the sense that it harked back not only to the confederated tribalism of the Celts and Northern Europeans, but also in its adherents' desire to return to the land, to identify with nature in more ancient ways, and to experience what we might term variants of gnosis, that is, of direct individual spiritual insight. One sees this in the attraction to Hindu and Buddhist gurus, but also in the significant role played by psychedelics during this era. All of these, like tribal music, are at least in part informed by a desire to go beyond the self-other division, to break beyond the objectification and self/other dualism that is the hallmark of modernity.

We see exactly these emphases in Theodore Roszak's seminal *The Making of a Counter Culture* (1969), the subtitle of which is *Reflections on the Technocratic Society and Its Youthful Opposition*. Deeply influenced by Jacques Ellul's pessimistic attacks on technocracy, Herbert Marcuse's *One-Dimensional Man* (1964), and Lewis Mumford's *The Myth of the Machine* (1967), Roszak's book emphasizes the role of Asian religions, poetry, magic, and mysticism in recovering aspects of humanity that are threatened by technicization of society.[102] Allen Ginsberg and Alan Watts are featured in the book's center. But the final chapter underscores the atavism of the era, and is particularly interesting in our context—it is a chapter on shamanism.

One might be surprised at the importance given to shamanism, given that the neoshamanic movement in the West was many years ahead yet. But this final chapter forecasts and calls for neoshamanism; it opposes to the "certification authority of state, corporation, university, or party," the "immediacy of personal vision" that like the "old magic" "could illuminate the sacramental presence in a tree, a pond, a rock, a totem."[103] The "instinctive fascination" of the counter-culture with magic, mysticism, and tribal lore represents a widespread effort to go to the root of the malaise afflicting contemporary society, to reconnect with the "ultimate ground of our existence," and to realize the autonomy of direct inner experience.[104]

Thus Roszak confirms the argument I am making here. The counter-culture represented the return of the archaic, which is also to say, the first sustained and widespread effort not to oppose modernity, but to invoke and realize in new ways previous suppressed, archaic ways of knowing and living that consist in the transcendence of the subject-object dualism inherent in modernity. Magic and mysticism are terms for efforts at exactly such transcendence, in the first instance of the objectified other, in the second of the isolated self. This argument is not that the counter-culture was necessarily successful in efforts to create a new culture, but rather that the effort to create a new culture would have to proceed along just these kinds of lines—that is, it would entail not merely changes in circumstances, but a fundamental reorientation of being, calling on ways of knowledge at once archaic and new. Such a reorientation is not anti-modern, but rather represents something fundamentally new, or renewed.

One could object that the counter-culture represented just another face of modernity, perhaps reactionary, but still in the end commodified and sold back as a simulacrum of itself. A case like this presumably would emphasize commercialism, the packaging of rock music, say, and would ignore as much as possible those countercultural aspects that I have emphasized. Such an argument is more or less the line pursued by Jameson and certainly by Baudrillard: it makes secular modernity a kind of möbius strip from which there is no escape, to which there is in the end no real alternative, similar to the amusing "neoconservative" hypothesis that secular modernity represents the "end of history." However, to believe modernity is an hermetically sealed end-state requires a willfully sustained historical naïveté.

The argument here—that the counter-culture represented a break with the prevailing religious and secular historical narratives of the West—we can describe in another way. The counter-culture represented the emergence into broader society of an essentially gnostic perspective, that is, a perspective that emphasizes above all not faith in an historical narrative promising a religious or secular millennium somewhere ahead, but direct individual spiritual insight here and now, exactly as Roszak insists. There is, of course, an American precedent for this, in the path marked out by Ralph Waldo Emerson, who in his first book, *Nature*, wrote that man as an individual need not resume his kingship by degrees, but should leap at once into the throne.[105] Emerson here, as often in his work, was asserting an American gnosis, that is, an assertion that spiritual insight is available to us now, not vicariously, but individually, directly, and immediately. What we see in the counter-culture—particularly where it is drawing on Buddhism and Hinduism just as Emerson himself was—is very much this kind of emphasis on gnosis.[106]

In the late 1960s counter-culture—informed by Zen Buddhism, Vedanta, Tibetan Buddhism, and other non-dualist religious traditions—is an explicit emphasis on "the mystical experience, the art experience, identity experience, unitive experience," that is, on non-duality, exactly as we saw in these remarks of Allen Ginsberg in 1967. *That* is what I am terming "gnosis," which does not imply an end-state of illumination, but rather an *inclination* away from subject-object dualism and toward subject-object unity. This gnostic tendency is what informs much of the counter-culture during this period. Such an observation should not be taken as a blanket valorization of the era or of its individual tendencies or charismatic figures, any more than it should be seen as a condemnation (which terms like "gnosis" usually are!). Rather, what I am suggesting here is meant as an initial foray into a broader understanding, not just of the counter-culture, but even more, of the central role that gnosis and its rejection continues to play in Western history and now in secular modern society.

Chapter Eleven

Towards New Cultures

When we consider the multiple crises of modernity—above all, the consumption and exhaustion of minerals, the soil, clean water, even the air, alongside the extraordinary growth of the human population, the development of ever more catastrophic weaponry, combined with the proclivity to war, to name only a few examples—one has to ask where any solutions might lie. What's more, as René Guénon recognized already early in the twentieth century, modernity is not static, but rather is accelerating in every respect, gathering technological speed and power. But this constantly growing technological power was not accompanied by any coordinated effort, indeed, even any visible effort at developing collective or individual wisdom.

Indeed, quite the opposite was evident in higher education, which increasingly was reduced to technical vocationalism. The humanities certainly had defenders during the first half of the twentieth century, at least, but by the end of that century, the humanities already were significantly diminished in scope and authority. Vocationalism was everywhere in the driver's seat. One didn't learn foreign languages along with literature any more; one instead learned a language in order to facilitate business communication. The study of literature was eclipsed by political ideology, abstract theorizing, and jargon; art was technicized into digital manipulation; philosophy became business or medical ethics, and so forth. The humanities no longer had the convictions of moral authority as the center of liberal higher education; increasingly, they were invaded by apostles of technicism, or were captured by those who saw themselves solely as cultural critics or even opponents.

It is true that in the late twentieth century one saw the "culture wars" in the United States, but truth be told, the "culture wars" were more of a minor skirmish between groups whose focus for the most part was narrowly political. On the one side were cultural critics motivated by what came to be known as "political correctness," and on the other side were the cultural conservatives, motivated by their reaction against "political correctness" in its various forms. The cultural critics attacked patriarchy; the cultural conservatives attacked the critics' "war against boys." The truth is, both sides made legitimate and even valuable arguments. But these arguments did not go very far; actually, they were effectively battling over a small piece of turf.

Neither the cultural critics nor the cultural conservatives were particularly interested in deeper questions. After all, political correctness and political incorrectness share most of the same assumptions—chiefly, that the political is paramount. But the political is actually a struggle for hegemony among competing interests, and takes place on an horizontal axis. One side harks backward, invoking the past; the other inveighs against the past while envisioning progress toward a more egalitarian future. Each side has legitimate points that nonetheless are limited in scope, defending or critiquing the American sociopolitical status quo as if it were the sum of culture rather than its absence.

One has to recognize that this series of skirmishes over political correctness or incorrectness took place in a larger cultural vacuum. Consumer society is not a culture; it is rather, the supplanting of cultures by industrial products, information packages, or entertainment. Missing from consumer society is the realization of depth and height; instead, one lives in a cornucopia of products, that is, of objects existing horizontally but not vertically. These objects are products to be used; they do not exist in a world that emerges from or that manifests the sacred. Products, resources, objects can be consumed—that is, used up. But that which is sacred cannot be treated in such a fashion.

A problem inherent in discussing even the possibility of new cultures is the prevailing truncation of the sacred, especially in those perspectives deriving from exoteric monolatry. By "truncation," I mean that the sacred is merely that which is prescribed out of a rigid doctrinal exoterism—the sacred is conceived as what is to be imposed on others by force. "God" is conceived as thoroughly other, and so too non-believers are perceived as completely other. "They" must be persuaded, converted, or forced to submit; and so society is seen through a lens of unforgiving moralizing.

All of these are characteristics of exoteric religion; and of course, secular modernity is also a kind of exoterism, since it derives from Judeo-Christian exoterism. The sacred in such cases is truncated inasmuch as the sense of union with nature, with the human, and with the divine is rendered impossible by the prevailing dualism.

Of course, there are different dimensions of the sacred, or perhaps one could say, different valences or modalities. Exoteric monotheism defines the sacred as that which reveals itself as dramatically other—which translates, in practical terms, into violence. God is what generates plagues or pestilences or hail or violent subjugation, what generates the most radical forms of otherness. This is true, certainly, of the Old Testament; and it is also certainly true of the Koran. As to the New Testament, it is not quite so clear. The original message of Christ has elements of radical otherness, to be sure—I come not to bring peace, but to bring the sword—yet the Sermon on the Mount, the parables, and injunctions to turn the other cheek, to be gentle as a lamb, to harm none and love all, these and their overarching message to forgive and to love others, such passages of the New Testament point toward or open into the possibility of esoterism.

When I refer to the possiblity of new cultures, then, I should be clear: I am not referring to exoterism giving birth to new monsters. We do not need more pseudo-paradises of proscription that, of course, turn out to be earthly hells; we do not need more Talibans or other fundamentalists generating radically prescriptive/proscriptive social orders. To put it another way: when I refer to new cultures, the very term "culture" carries esoteric connotations. Culture is not a collection of proscriptions; it is not imposed by force; it is, rather, the natural manifestation of an esoteric center, at the heart of which is the possibility of union with the divine. A culture carries within it and expresses the possibility of gnosis, that is, of inner illumination of the individual. I am pointing toward esoterism as central because this is the most crucial element of culture; it is indeed its ultimate purpose.[108]

What follows is an outline of what is essential for a new culture, a metaphysics of new cultures, if you will. Such a metaphysics is, at heart, non-theistic, in the sense that even in theistic traditions, it centers on the theme of union, that is, of non-dualism. The metaphysical architecture of cultures does not depend upon whether the exoteric dimensions of the particular tradition are monotheistic, polytheistic, or non-theistic. These outward characteristics in fact can be combined in a single current, as is the case in Tibetan Buddhism, for example, which features a plethora of deities, and yet for all that, remains non-theistic. One finds a similar dynamic in the Christian *via negativa* mysticism of Dionsyius the Areopagite and Meister Eckhart: these figures are paradigmatic for esoteric nondual non-theism existing inside a broader religious tradition characterized by exoteric (dualistic) Christian theism. Likewise, one finds Sufism in Islam and Kabbalah in Judaism as esoteric mystical currents borne along within the broader waters of exoteric monotheism.

A nondual gnostic centrum is essential to the emergence of new cultures. Without that center, the new culture necessarily would be only an exoteric imposition upon others, exactly what is characteristic of the social structures that generated the multiple crises of modernity. As we have already seen, industrial modernity in all of its various guises is dualistic. For a new culture to take root and flourish, it cannot derive from the same premises as modernity. We have already seen that what became modernity was present already in the Old Testament, and later in the suppression of gnosis in what became prevailing dualistic Christianity in late antiquity. The roots of new cultures must sink, therefore into different soil and aquifers; they must go deeper, and to different sources than those from which modernity emerged and flourished.

It is not that new cultures must simply reject technology and industrial modernity, as primitivists like John Zerzan would have it. New cultures do not emerge from reaction or rejection, because reaction or rejection, however noble the impulses that guide them, do not sink roots; they exist on a horizontal plane, extolling an idealized past along the lines that we also see in many traditionalists, who are reacting bitterly against the present. There is much in the past to be revered and drawn upon—do not misunderstand me here. But archaism has the inevitable result of disempowering the future, and giving rise to a sense of futility, a belief that grand historical forces make virtually impossible anything but a decline into a dark age of dissolution. No enduring new culture, in the way we are envisioning it here, can emerge from a dualistic basis.

Rather, authentically new cultures will need an esoteric, non-dualistic center out of which they can develop and ultimately flower. This is because the gnostic center is inclusive rather than exclusive; its cultural manifestations are not fear-driven violence, but kindness and concern for others. A non-dualistic center means that the culture does not revolve around notions of domination or military/industrial expansion and control of nature and of other people. It does not proceed out of adversarial assumptions.[109] Non-dualism, in its very nature, is of a different order than dualistic power; its premises and its consequences follow from a shared awareness of the underlying unity of oneself and others, and of oneself and the natural world.

Of course, critics of this line of thought will argue that humanity is fallen and destructive by nature; that one cannot have a new culture based upon new premises; that such a notion amounts to a kind of Aristophanian cloud-cuckooland; that utopias cannot come into being; that humanity is bound to an adversarial relationship with both other peoples and with nature; and that war and military-industrial assaults on the world are inevitable as a result of intrinsic human pathology; that in effect, one can only proceed from the intellectual architecture that brought the modern world into being as it is in the first place.

But we know, from the existence of other possibilities within human history, that there were and are myriad alternatives to modern military-industrial monosociety. Merely because a Hobbesian view prevailed in the West, and an Althusian view was neglected, if not outright suppressed, does not mean that therefore an Althusian perspective is wrong or untenable. Indeed, as it becomes increasingly clear that the military-industrial model—based on antagonism, consumption, and destruction—cannot endure, alternatives necessarily will begin to emerge. To insist that they will not emerge is to accept an entirely pessimistic view of human possibility. Such a view leads inexorably into the ultimate pessimism and cynicism of the totalized state, that is, the Behemoth state that "protects" its citizens or denizens by controlling, imprisoning, torturing, and executing them in order to enforce exoteric, dualistic political dogmas.[110] My argument here is that alternatives are not just possible, but essential. However, these alternatives, to be enduring and meaningful, need to proceed from different premises than modernity, or they will only produce variants of it.

A new culture could be envisaged as a sphere radiating out from a centerpoint. That nondual centerpoint is gnosis, or direct knowledge of nonduality. The center of the culture, then, consists in those who have most completely realized knowledge of nonduality; they are the cultural elders or guides. Such an individual is recognizable by other such individuals, and this recognition is what forms the guiding council of the culture. The guiding council emerges by group consensus to encourage leadership by those who are not self-interested, and who are motivated by wisdom that is recognized by others in the community.

Here, the term "culture" refers to a relatively small local or regional group—perhaps tribal or a tribal confederation—but not to large, artificial constructions like nations or states. A new culture is indigenous, in that it emerges organically out of a particular landscape and people, and its gnostic center is what keeps it from selfish and destructive behavior. This is not a minor point. Localism and regionalism are prerequisities to emerging new cultures; new cultures emerge from the center outward, reaching a local equilibrium that remains stable and that does not expand into imperial, centralist tendencies. Gargantuan, abstract nation-state or imperial constructs result by their very nature in the opposite of the kinds of new cultures we envisage here.

It is vital that new cultures have a nondual, gnostic center, but it is also vital that they express themselves through beauty, that is, through craftsmanship. We can recognize an emerging culture by its arts, that is, by the beauty of what its artisans create, which in turn reflects the particularities of that locality and region. Coastal cultures, forest cultures, alpine cultures, each emerge out of particular landscapes and out of the recognition of particular deities or spirits that correspond to those landscapes. There is, in other words, an archaic dimension to the emergence of cultures, which is what we see when we visit an indigenous American petroglyph site in the rockface outcroppings high above a river. Those petroglyphs represent the cultural record of encounters with nonhuman beings, whether one wishes to call them spirits or deities. Here we see the manifestation of archaic art, the wellspring of perennially renewed encounters in nature with the archaic and with nonhuman intelligence. That is culture at its sparest, purest form.

Characteristic of secular modernity is a severe disjunct between humanity and nature, symbolized, for instance, by a huge earthmover, a grader or a bulldozer that indiscriminately pushes away the soil and all that grows and lives on and in it. This is profoundly different than the indigenous view (belonging, after all, to indigenous Europeans too) that there are spirits manifesting themselves in nature, and especially in sacred places. In other words, in the view of ancient Celts or Norse tribes, nature is not opaquely "other," but transparent, even translucent in sacred places, so that the human, natural, and spirit worlds are fluid and intermingled.

A new culture will regenerate some of this interconnectedness between humanity, nature, and spirits. This is not to say that a new culture is necessarily shamanic, but most likely it will have shamanic elements or aspects. Shamanism is not by nature in conflict with a culture's nondual center, but rather could be seen as an expression of it, so that the two—shamanism and non-dualism together—act to perpetually renew the culture that continues to change and develop even as it remains in equipoise, that is, not going off in aggressive or destructive directions that result from what we may term the dualistic temptation.

What might such a new culture look like? For one thing, it will eschew gigantism. Its reach and its aims would be modest and local. Both the shamanic and the nondual aspects of the culture represent an inner, experiential emphasis that naturally entails less outwardness and desire for acquisitions or power. It will be somewhat tribal, because tribes form the most natural of human associations. Because the West has long tended toward dispersed monogamous extended families in individual or extended familial houses or enclaves, one can expect that such arrangements would be common.

And how would such a culture protect itself? Let us say that there is a more communal dimension to these tribal groups than is present in modernity. How would these dispersed tribes and their communities defend themselves from marauders? The answer is in confederacy, that is, in mutual protective associations, exactly as Althusius outlined in *Politica*. Really, the only essential function of a confederacy is mutual protection, and this is precisely what we still see reflected at least to some extent in the Swiss confederation today. The individual local or regional tribes band together in order to assure by mutual agreement that when they are threatened, they will respond together.

The beauty of such an arrangement is precisely that in it, the power remains with the tribes and communities, whose elders and guides concede authority to the confederacy only for purposes of mutual protection, and then only on the basis of consensus. This arrangement is, of course, the inverse of the modern secular bureaucratic state, where the centralized government and its authorities constantly accrue more and more power at the expense of localities and regions. Whereas the modern bureaucratic state tends automatically toward authoritarianism and indeed toward state totalism, the decentralized confederacy by its very nature acts as a permanent counter to this tendency, and yet it allows for mutual protection.

What we are envisioning here, of course, is an entirely different way of understanding the nature and purpose of humanity and politics in relation to nature. Virtually everything in modernity—that is, in military-industrial society—went in the other direction, toward gigantism and centralism of power, accompanied by cultural fragmentation and dissolution. Here, we foresee precisely the opposite: that is, the decentralization of power and the strengthening of local and regional cultural and political authority. But whereas in the military-industrial model political power is foremost, and culture takes a back seat or is destroyed, here culture is foremost, and political power is subordinated to it.

And culture emerges locally, out of the unique combination of people and their familiar landscapes, organically and, to use an Althusian word, symbiotically. Because culture is foremost, the political drive for power is controlled, harnessed to cultural and ultimately to religious aspirations whose expression is wisdom, that is, it is altruistic. This altruism is not limited only to people, or particular people, but is opened outward to include also animals, plants, the natural world, all beings. This is the foundation of the organic and symbiotic nature of what I am calling here emergent culture.

The bearers of culture are the elders, the solons who serve not only as guides or guardians, but as the incarnations and transmitters of the culture. Whereas in military-industrial society, those who are most clever and devious are most often rewarded, in these emergent new cultures, what is most valued is wisdom. That is because the metaphysics of the new cultures is non-dualistic, that is, the new culture represents both the aspiration to wisdom and the expression of it, rather than the dualistic aspiration to power and the expression of it. This new model of culture emerges out of its metaphysical basis in non-dualism: at least ideally, the solons are those who are most selfless, that is, most altruistic, altruism being the practical expression of non-dualism.

Altruism also is the protection against what some seem to fear about non-dualism—that it may lead to antinomianism, to a willy-nilly rejection of all established order. Of course, examples of this are rather hard to come by, as it turns out. And what protects against antinomian disorder is an altruistic *nomos* or cultural order that derives from and reflects a non-dualist metaphysical center. Antinomianism is precisely that: anti-nomos, a rejection of a rigid social order that has become sclerotic. But if the *nomos* is already flexible, growing organically out of a cultural unity whose center is beyond friend/foe dualism, then the nomos/antinomos dualism is unnecessary. A *nomos* based in altruism is hardly likely to encourage destructive acts or whatever else might be seen as resulting from the often-phantom "antinomianism."

But this altruism extends beyond the human realm to include also the non-human. One consequence of a nondual metaphysics is that the

126

human is not seen as against the non-human; rather, the paradigm is closer to what we see in agrarianism or, if we were to look to the East, in Taoism. That is, the emergent new cultures arising from a nondual metaphysics are, practically speaking, much closer to a village-agrarian countryside than to a modern urban-industrial system. In the village-agrarian landscape, most people grow or raise much of their own food, or purchase it from neighbors; there are woods nearby; and most things that one needs come from local farmers, fishers, hunters, or craftsmen.

At this point, of course, we begin to see some of the practical dimensions of what I am terming emergent cultures. What is necessary here is not a manifesto or some process or system that could be imposed upon people—we have seen enough of those and their dire consequences during the twentieth century—nor a revolutionary impulse, for that matter. Rather, we are outlining different aspects of what must emerge symbiotically out of particular places and peoples as part of a larger cultural renaissance. Such a renascence can be inspired, it can be tended, encouraged, but it has to emerge, ultimately, from people themselves, not as some kind of ideological construct, but out of a lived and integral communal and individual spirit. What we turn to now is the culmination of our discussion in what we term the mystical state.

Chapter Twelve

The Mystical State

A term like "the mystical state," however clever, is bound to elicit unease, because it encapsulates in itself exactly what is ignored, indeed, eclipsed in modernity. After all, am I, with such a phrase, encouraging mysticism? Am I imagining that a society might be center around mysticism? What a strange idea! What could that possibly mean? My meaning is obscure, in a dualistic, technological world built by the quantification and manipulation of all that surrounds us. Perhaps the technological edifice will be shattered by its own successes in the end, but still, even if the technological era is followed by a "dark age," we have a hard time imagining how mysticism might offer any benefits to the Hobbesian denizens of that benighted time to come. And yet. Allow me the liberty of what you may think a mere pipe dream, here.

Throughout this book, we have alluded to Gnosticism and the early Christian era because I have come to believe that there we find the decisive period in which what we now term secular modernity has its origins. What I have suggested is that if Basilides had prevailed, if Christianity had not taken a tragic turn toward dualism and its companion, exoterism, if negative theology had remained central rather than having been mostly marginalized, we might have seen a very different historical trajectory. Indeed, secular modernity itself might not have come into being in the way that it did. But in a way, all of that is water under the bridge: it cannot be brought back.

Hence, our other theme: that of emergent cultures. We have looked back through history in order to trace back where things went wrong, but also to find precedents for understanding alternative political and

129

religious models. These precedents in turn offer ways to understand what I am terming emergent cultures, ways to envision not just the reform of this or that aspect of technological society, but entirely different ways of being in the world. New ways of being in the world require not just tinkering or outward confections, but a metaphyics that can serve as the center of the new cultures. For that, we will not turn to Basilides, or indeed to any of the Christian authors with whom I have always felt a certain kinship. Rather, we will turn to a metaphysics independent of the esoteric/exoteric dynamics that characterize the Abrahamic traditions, and a metaphysics at the center of what I term the mystical state.

This metaphysics was present in the period of late antiquity, parallel to the Jewish and Christian religious currents, yet separate from them. It is important for us because it provides a philosophical and religious understanding that does not necessarily conflict with monotheism, and yet is not bound up with it and all its baggage. Furthermore, although it provides an intellectual framework, it is not dogmatic or ideological but experimental, adaptable to new approaches and perspectives. This metaphysics is, of course, Neoplatonic.

Now conventionally, the words "mysticism" or "mystical" are used in such vague, wooly ways that one really cannot tell what is meant by them, so it will be useful here to set out what we mean. Here, the term "mystical" refers to a gnostic process of inner awakening that leads to the realization of transcendence. Mysticism describes the inner process whereby one realizes what is described or at least hinted or gestured at in metaphysical descriptions, which are more or less cartographic representations deriving from direct inner experience. The greatest of the Neoplatonists, Plotinus, offered an exhaustively detailed metaphysics in his series of treatises compiled under the name *Enneads*, and what follows draws upon his work, but also upon the works of Porphyry, Iamblichus, Proclus, and Damascius.

The essential, the indispensable aim of human life is to realize one's identity with transcendence, which can also be characterized as gnosis. The problem with these or any other terms is in the very nature of such labels: they become conceptually reified and immediately form barriers to rather than vehicles of understanding or realization. Hence one can refer to the Transcendent, or the One, but then these words themselves become like objects, objectifications of what is unobjectifiable, indeed, is unobjectification itself. This is the problem that Plotinus constantly confronted, and we can see him offering first one approach, then another, occasionally even remarking explicitly on how if this particular explication does not work for the hearer/reader, he may need to offer another one.

We also can describe this aim as the ascent from dualistic consciousness—that is, objectifying consciousness existing in self/other relationship with what is perceived through the senses—toward the transcendence of self/other. This transcendence is perceived not through discursive reason but through the intuitive sense, which we can term noesis. Noesis is not exactly the same as what is usually conveyed by the term "intellectual," because noesis in its lesser aspect is a direct perception of the principles or essences that transcend the physical world. The mutable world is, of course, in constant flux by very definition, whereas noesis is direct perception of what transcends mutability.

Noesis ultimately is not perception of what is outside oneself, but rather perception of what is also within oneself—it must be within, in some sense, in order for it to be perceptible through noesis. The very possibility of noesis is itself testimony, if we can put it that way, to the inner identity of self and transcendence, or to put it another way, to the inner capacity of the self opening up into transcendence, the act of perception of which is noesis. Noesis is key because it is the faculty and act of perception of what is already present both within oneself and within the cosmos; noesis is both conduit and that which is conveyed.

Noesis is the process by which the individual realizes or awakens to these successively more transcendent spheres or realms, or for that matter, to what we are terming here the fundamental field of the not-ground. Noesis is not identical with intellectuality—rather, noesis includes and transcends what conventionally is referred to as "intellectual." Noesis, or noesis, is unitive, in that it refers not merely to knowledge-of, that is to perception of something external to oneself, but to knowing-through-identity. Noesis is awareness that unites both the knower and that which is known.

The purpose of a living culture is to encourage noesis in those who are so inclined. Noesis is a conduit through which new cultures are born; it is the conduit to what transcends the sensible world, and ultimately to what transcends all form, shape, or differentiation. We could use the term "intuition," but intuition implies something like mere precognition, that is, perceptions about the sensible realm in the future, whereas noesis is of a different order entirely. Noesis is living awareness of what transcends and illuminates the sensible realm, up through the supernal orders, the principles or powers of which the sensible world is only a reflection, up to inexpressible transcendence. A culture is born, enlivened, and sustained by direct contact with the supersensible, but especially with the inexpressible, the not-this, not-that.

We could describe it in the following way: the transcendent not-ground is the fundamental field within which all existence takes place. Within this not-ground, we could imagine a circle or sphere, and then concentric spheres within that, at the center of which is the material or sensible world. Each of these concentric spheres could be described as akin to successive dampings-down of an electrical current, and the physical world at the center of these is the "furthest" from the fundamental field of the not-ground, even though the not-ground is present everywhere and at all times. But sensibility obscures this fundamental field of unity, sensibility draws us outward into differentiation, or perceptions of "outwardness." The reverse is also true: concentric spheres, as one moves toward the transcendent field of the not-ground, are successively less explicable or describable by discursive reason, which is most applicable to the sphere of sensory differentiation.

Discursive logic is valuable, no doubt of it. Instrumentalizing reason or discursive logic are what make possible the astonishing technological achievements that are the hallmark of modernity. Logic is, however, binary: it works inexorably in a sequential manner, and seeks to divide the cosmos into this and that, into ever finer distinctions, thereby the better to understand and to manipulate it. These logical distinctions concern the sphere of sensory differentiation, and they remain dualistic in their very nature. Machinery is the outward expression and perfection of this dualistic instrumentalization; logic is the inner structure of instrumental machinery. Logic is the engine of exoterism.

But noesis includes and goes beyond logic because it is recognition of identity, or to be more accurate, unicity. Unicity is experienced union— the term is a dynamic expression of what Plotinus termed "the One." Noesis is our human capacity to participate in or to realize our unicity, and another, though less precise or accurate term for the process leading to this intellective realization, is contemplation.[111] Contemplation/noesis includes logic, but it goes beyond it because it enters into the metaphysical realm where subject and object no longer are perceived as separated.

What I am envisioning here are new cultures that emerge out of the noesis of those who are capable of giving shape to what they understand from their direct immersion in timelessness or eternity. These new cultures are the outward expressions of inward realization. Those whose lives are devoted to noesis are the new culture's elders and guardians, its creators and sustainers. And of course, since the aim of the culture as a whole is the same as its origin, that is, noesis, it is to this end that the educational and social system is oriented. This means that the new cultures entail new forms of education, as well as a new politics guided by those who are devoted to noesis and its altruistic fruition in the world.

There is no intrinsic reason why new cultures could not develop around an altruistic rather than a selfish orientation. Such an orientation is there already in every society, because it is nascent in most people. One thinks, here, of Peter Kropotkin's theory of evolution based on mutual benefit or cooperation—it expresses a perspective rather different than the one emphasized by Darwinism, but one that also has validity. Just because military-industrial-technological society developed in an atmosphere of competitive exploitation and aggression does not mean that is the only possible ethos. Required is a voluntary, comprehensive socio-cultural reorientation toward altruism.

Some will assert that such a reorientation is impossible, but there are historical instances offering tantalizing hints that other ways of being are possible. One such example is the patron saint of Switzerland, Nicholas von Flüe (1417-1487), known colloquially still as "Brother Klaus." Most Westerners have never heard of this remarkable figure, but he remains an important, even defining historic figure within Switzerland, for reasons that will soon become clear.

Brother Klaus lived his whole life in a little valley called "the Ranft," in what is now central Switzerland. The roughhewn wooden farmhouse in which he was born still stands, and one can visit the chapel and meditation cell that he had built along the banks of the stream that flows through the valley below the village that today is called Flüeli-Ranft. One can walk down the path from the village, along the edge of the valley, and down to the chapel, accompanied by the sound of the rushing brook, while nearby one might hear the clang of a churchbell from the village or from a more distant monastic outpost. The wooded mountainous region is still shrouded in stillness and sanctity invoked centuries before by the extraordinary figure known as Brother Klaus.

Nicholas von Flüe was born to Heinrich and Hemma, and to a freeheld farming family in the forest district of Obwalden. Already by this time the Swiss confederation long since had formed (in 1291), and Nicholas's family's land lay in the center of it, in what is known as *Ur-Schweiz*, or "primordial Switzerland." This is high country, with many independent farms, and much fishing and hunting, forest and rushing streams, where oftentimes the mountaintops are shrouded in clouds. The Swiss were known as a warrior people, who were quick to defend their confederation, but keen to preserve each area's independence. Nicholas's family, like most families in this region, had an established history there.

Nicholas, we are told in depositions taken after his death, was a singularly devout and solitary boy, often inclined to slip away and pray behind a shed or in the woods. When he was sixteen, he had a vision of a meditation tower on the western bank of the local valley stream, where in fact one day he had built his chapel and meditation cell. But this was a time of war, and he was called up for military service; indeed, he is said to have fought in a number of battles during the 1440s. But he is also said to have prayed for both sides to be kept safe, and counseled clemency for captives and for the defeated.

Despite his eremitic inclination, Nicholas married Dorothea Wyes, and with her had ten children. By all indications, it was a happy marriage, though Nicholas spent many days fasting and praying, often in contemplation while herding or watching cattle in the alpine pastureland. Increasingly, Nicholas felt the pull of the hermit's life, and in October, 1467, he obtained Dorothea's unwilling permission, and left home in order to lead a lay eremitic life elsewhere. But on his journey, he say a distant town lit with an unsettling reddish glow, and he felt called to return home to the Ranft, where he knew he belonged. There he stayed, eventually in a meditation cell. Long a faster, after his return to the Ranft, he was said to have gone without food for eleven days, then for years at a time.

Nicholas's fame grew, and eventually people came to check on him to see whether he was secretly being fed by someone in his family or a neighbor, but no one could be found doing so. Such feats are also reputed of Tibetan hermits or yogis, who also retreat into the wilderness in order to intensify their religious practice. In Nicholas's case, he remained relatively close to his family, and to his native town, so word of what he was doing and why spread quite quickly. He became regionally famous as a hermit, and people often came to him for personal advice or for blessing.

It is because of his most famous advice that Nicholas became known not only as "Brother Klaus" but as the *pater patriae* of Switzerland—the father of his country. Nicholas, or Brother Klaus, from early on in his reclusion, became a source of advice and guidance not only for individuals, but for the whole region. Hence, when it appeared that civil war would break out in central Switzerland in December, 1481, it was to the hermit Nicholas that a worried priest urgently came in order to obtain his advice to the potentially warring parties. Such was the intractibility of the conflict that it might have meant the end of the Swiss confederation itself. But Klaus sent a message that persuaded both sides to reconcile, and indeed, to produce the Covenant of Stans, a prototype of Swiss constitutional law.

A figure like Brother Klaus, the patron saint of Switzerland, exemplifies the kind of relationship between reclusion and politics that is possible, and that in fact can have profound influence. The character of Switzerland itself still today can be seen in the life of Brother Klaus: his willingness to go to war, but his desire to avoid it; his agrarian community; his neutrality and refusal to be caught up in the dialectics of one side against another; his love of life in the wild mountains. It is not that these characteristics are unique to Klaus alone—quite the opposite. In many respects, these characteristics distinguish Switzerland as a whole, and indeed, even today Switzerland retains them in one way or another.

Klaus, off in his high valley fasting and praying, nonetheless was very much a part of his community and region, very much a spiritual and political guide, not because he wanted power, but precisely because he eschewed it. This kind of relationship between the yogi or recluse and the polis is often held to belong more to Eastern than to Western peoples, more to Taoism or Buddhism than to Christianity. And of course that is true, broadly speaking. There are not so many Brother Klauses in Western history. Yet there are some, and their existence and influence is suggestive of further possibilities. In its confederational polis, in its combination of agrarian and town cultures, in a host of ways, Switzerland represents a model for the kind of future I am envisioning here.

Such a model is not a pipe dream. The examples of Brother Klaus and of Switzerland are quite real. I do not offer them as exemplary in every way, but as evidence of possibility.[112] What would happen if more people were to come together with the individual and collective will to move in this other direction, with an emphasis more on inner than on outer life, more on spiritual illumination than on temporal power? Here, I am not referring to some grand social movement, which one has to distrust from the outset, but to a local and indigenous, one may say, autochthonous turn, perhaps along the lines that we saw in the communalism of the late 1960s, where people of like mind gather together and begin to live a different life. The example of Brother Klaus shows that not even a communal endeavor is necessary, only a remarkable individual. New cultures will begin, not from anyone's grand design, but from the first steps of new Brother Klauses.

135

Conclusion

Every book is an adventure, as much for its author as for its readers. In *The Mystical State*, we have ventured into mostly uncharted territory, and the result has been a foundational book, one that outlines the terrain and that offers not only a sense of where we have been and how we got to where we are, but also a sense of which directions we might go, and which course might be most beneficial. I realize that some, perhaps even all of this book represents unfamiliar figures and ideas for most people, but after all, that's the idea. There's no point in trudging over the same rutted paths again and again. It is true that there are many books published these days, but this is the only one that forges into this new and unfamiliar landscape. It is the landscape of possibility, of a renewed future, of new cultures. Now that you've nearly finished, prepare to start over, to reconsider it again. There's more here than meets the eye on the first impression.

For convenience's sake, perhaps we might look over the new vistas and reconsider their significances now. First, there is the question of how we came to where we are today. Those who have traced the emergence of military-industrial-technological society back to the Bible, beginning in many respects with the seminal essay of Lynn White, are on to something. What I have termed exoterism is indeed a signal legacy of monotheism or monolatry, and it is to exoterism that modern technological society is most indebted. Exoterism is an insistence on the control or conversion of others; it is exoterism that demands the sacred places of other peoples be destroyed, that every one of them be killed, that to "cleanse" one's community and to make it "worthy" in the eyes of its god, one must track down the impure, the heretical, the "others" on the inside that correspond to the "others" on the outside.

What I am suggesting, in other words, is continuity between the dualism inherent in the monolatric traditions, and the dualism that is the engine of technological rationalism. Secular modernity is throughout indebted to and a product of dualistic ways of understanding, and this is clearest in its most pathological forms, the political religions like communism and national socialism. Inquisitional pathologies rapidly developed in the totalitarianisms of the twentieth century because their seeds were already present; religious dualism gave birth to political dualism along the historical lines described at length in *The New Inquisitions*. This is not to say that such pathologies are limited to the West, or to the patrimony of the monolatric traditions, only that, even though many may not want to face this matter squarely, the fact is that we can trace this continuity from antiquity to the present, and it is important that we do so. We need to see how modernity emerged, what its ancient origins are, and what alternatives might exist.

This is not to say that modernity is without its blessings, despite the destruction it leaves in its wake. I am not inveighing against all technologies here, nor am I arguing that everything modernity has produced is irredeemable. Far from it. For all its drawbacks, technology also bestows its gifts, and there is often a kind of steely poetic beauty to those gifts. Man has created machines to accomplish any task one might imagine, produced alternative visionary worlds, achieved feats that almost seem to be magical. At the same time, the technological system as a whole is voracious; it and its adherents seem unable to stop devouring every bit of oil, all of the coal, everything that can be used up; unable also to cease poisoning the water and the air; or to end the extinction of countless animal, plant, and marine species.

I am suggesting that when we look back into that remarkable period of late antiquity, when Judaism, Christianity, and then Islam were formed, we can see that especially in Christianity, there was very clearly a road not taken, indeed, a road the entrance to which was blocked. What's worse, those who had gone down that road were mostly vilified. To understand this is already to begin to realize what we can learn from history or counterhistory. And when we consider that other road in more detail, a road with many branches and one leading into what is for us mostly uncharted virginal territory, we have to ask, we are compelled to ask, what if? What would be the implications of gnosis or noesis for us, or for a future polis, for future new cultures?

There are two authors whose work is particularly important in answering such questions: Basilides and Plotinus. Basilides offers the essence, the center of this alternative form of early Christianity, one most akin to the *Prajnaparamita Sutra* tradition in Buddhism. The non-dualism of Basilides stands in stark contrast to what developed in "orthodox" forms of Christianity, the most extreme dualistic form of which ultimately was the Inquisitional apparatus in the Roman West. It is no accident that Basilides created no institutional legacy as a carapace over the fascia of doctrinal formulations: he and his school represents an esoteric, initiatic tradition uninterested in socio-political or institutional hegemony. And Plotinus offers a metaphysics with a non-dualist pinnacle or center. In Plotinus, we see in detail the non-dualist metaphysics whose implications incorporate the possibility of what I am terming here a mystical state.

When we turn from metaphysics to practical application, we turn to the idea of subsidiarity, that is, to a dispersed, agrarian, localist model that arises more or less indigenously. Subsidiarity is associated with Catholicism, but it has a Protestant history as well, most notably in the *Politica* of Johannes Althusius. The central idea of this ancient Western political model is straightforwardly that what can be dealt with at a private or local level, should be, and that political life ought to be based on voluntary association, that is, on the family and extended family, on the local and regional neighborhoods. Centralized authority arises from the voluntary association of regions for clearly overarching matters like collective military security of a commonwealth or confederation. In this confederalist model, political authority belongs primarily to the individual, family, and locality, and only secondarily, by derivation, to any larger, voluntary confederation of localities, which can be disbanded by secession. Such a confederate model Althusius termed "symbiotic," and the voluntary associations that comprise the confederacy he termed a "symbiosis."

Symbiosis well describes what we have in mind as characteristic of these emergent cultures of the future. Here, however, symbiosis refers not only to human beings living together, but also to the larger communities that include animals, birds, plants, the earth, mountains, water, air, spirits, gods or celestial beings—that is, visible and invisible communities of all who surround us. The particularities of cultures emerge autochthonously, from individual landscapes and communities, and are not imposed by fiat from above, legislative or otherwise. A symbiotic and localist orientation is essential in order to avoid what we may call the dualistic temptation, that is, the objectifying and dualistic inclinations that generated technocratic society, from which almost everything symbiotic is excluded except for a select group of humans.

The human community is governed by *collegia*, that is, colleges of colleagues who belong to particular professions or trades, and beyond the colleges or guilds, by representative elders in council. The community is agrarian because, historically, this is the most stable social basis: it means that food is local and regional, not dependent on transport from distant lands, and it provides for an economic foundation upon which the other trades, building, roads, and so forth can be built. Some communities may belong more to oceans or lakes than to the inlands, but the cultural organization is similar: it develops organically and voluntarily out of the immediate locality and its guilds or colleges of trades and professions. This is exactly the kind of cultural realm described by Wilhelm Röpke, exemplified most of all by his beloved Switzerland. It is entirely possible. We could easily imagine the Republic of Vermont as such a place, for instance.

Some might argue that such a confederated, agrarian, dispersed culture would be static, "backward," not dynamic and chaotic like global abstract hypercapitalist corporatism. And of course, this would be true. Such a confederated agrarian culture *would* be much more static—that is, stable—than we see in hypercapitalism, where everything is oriented toward consumption, toward using everything up as fast as possible, toward immediate abstract financial profit, toward destruction of the land, of animals, of plants, of whatever can be converted from a stable into a consumed and ruined state, thereby adding to one's personal monetary aggrandizement. A localized agrarian culture of the kind we are envisioning here would be oriented toward continuity, toward preservation, toward higher values than mere financial exploitation.

It is entirely possible for such a dispersed, agrarian culture to be prosperous and relatively egalitarian at the same time, not least precisely because it is a culture, that is to say, it has a religious center and orientation. Such a culture has an orientation beyond itself, that is, beyond self-aggrandizement; it is oriented toward at least the possibility of individual self-transcendence. This is the practical consequence of the non-dualist metaphysics with which we began. Such a metaphysics infuses the culture with at least the possibility of self-transcendence as a shared aim of human life, as a shared orientation. It opens up the culture to the contemplative path as a central possibilty of human life, as furthermore a vocation and avocation to be revered and respected. Such a culture can be prosperous and egalitarian precisely because there is this contemplative dimension and orientation built into it, reminding folk that there is more to life than wealth or power, that indeed, the ultimate aims of human life are inner realizations, not outer accumulations that cannot be held onto or brought through the gate of death anyway.

What we are calling the mystical state—in both the individual and communal senses of the term—is realizable. It represents the primary alternative to centralized hypercapitalism and its successors or companions, authoritarian and even totalitarian regimes. The mystical state is decentralized, rooted in the ancient Western values of familial and communal identity, individual liberty, and altruism, not greed, kindness, not cruelty, and voluntarism, not tyranny. The mystical state, in both senses, is prefigured in Nicholas von Flüe, or Brother Klaus, and in the agrarian communal Switzerland where he lived. He represents the mystical current within Catholicism visible also in earlier, more well known mystics like Meister Eckhart and Johannes Tauler, but in a socio-cultural and political context not too far from what we are envisioning here as a future possibility.

We cannot yet see in detail the particular forms that the mystical state will take, because its particularities depend upon the confluence of individuals with an individual landscape in an emergent culture. Nonetheless, we can see quite clearly the general outlines of these emergent cultures. They will have at their centers a non-dualist metaphysics that is both their inspiration and their protection against the dangers and temptations posed by dualism, especially in its more virulent forms. And they will express themselves according to the dispositions of particular tribes, regions, and confederacies, reflecting and working with the contours of their particular natural niches. In some places, people will acknowledge many gods and spirits; in others, people may be more inclined toward an explicit non-dualism of the kind one sees in Zen Buddhism. The mystical state expresses and embraces heterogeneity and heterodoxy within an overarching shared metaphysics.

It is vital that we begin now to envision new, yet ancient ways of living. We live in a time of dramatic crises, a period of ascendent authoritarianism and state totalism, and yet paradoxically of the dissolution of centralism in every sphere, but in particular, in religion, economy, and politics. The forces of centralism that seek to continue to hold sway, and the forces of dissolution, these are arrayed against one another more starkly than ever before. Will we continue to exploit and lay waste to the natural world? Will we continue in the dualistic course laid down already millennia ago? Or can we now begin to envision new ways of life, the development of cultures whose ultimate aim is not outward domination, but inner life and illumination?

What we can imagine, can become real. It is possible to envision the kind of emergent culture alluded to in this book, and indeed, I believe it is essential that we continue to develop such a vision, to look forward, beyond the immediate catastrophes caused by the shortsightedness of what has come to be known as "modernity," toward what is possible. Because to imagine it is already to have made it possible. Here, we are foreseeing new cultures that are rooted not in history as it is usually conveyed, but in counterhistory. This new house will be built upon the cornerstones that the former builders rejected; its ancestors are figures like Basilides and Plotinus, and its center is not dualism but non-dualism, its motivation not the horizontal desire to vanquish or annihilate the other, but the vertical longing for union that expresses itself in the loving unity of a living culture.

It is no doubt true that there is a long history of prejudice in the West against a word like "mysticism," let alone against a phrase like "the mystical state." But there is also a long history of unactualized potential in what these words convey. As "modernity" fails, as authoritarians seek more and more power to "make things like they were," it is critically important to keep our eyes focused not on the mug's reactionary game, but on the living alternatives represented in a phrase like "the mystical state." Stable, emergent cultures that respect the natural world and its indigenous spirits, that are oriented toward the realization of noesis, that develop beautiful art and living expressions of cultural vitality—if we can envision them, then they already are alive and growing, and it is our task to nourish them. This is our hope for the future, hinted at in the communal polis of the past, still to come to fruition one day.

Notes

1 See Karen King, *What is Gnosticism?* (Cambridge; Harvard UP, 2003), p. 226.
2 Ibid., pp. 12-13.
3 See Hans Blumenberg, Robert Wallace, trs., *The Legitimacy of the Modern Age* (Cambridge: MIT, 1983), pp. 125 ff.
4 Ibid., p. 126.
5 Ibid., p. 137.
6 See, for example, Ilse Bulhof and Laurens ten Kate, *Flight of the Gods: Philosophical Perspectives on Negative Theology*, (New York: Fordham UP, 2000); see also J.P. Williams, *Denying Divinity*, (New York: Oxford UP, 2000).
7 From William Blake, "The Everlasting Gospel."
8 See Johann Baptist Metz, *A Passion for God: The Mystical-Political Dimension of Christianity*, (New York: Paulist Press, 1998), p. 154.
9 Ibid., p. 163.
10 The comparison of Buddhism and Gnosticism has a significant history. See, for instance, J. Kennedy, "Buddhist Gnosticism, the System of Basilides," in *Journal of the Royal Asiatic Society*, (1902): 377-415; Gilles Quispel, "Gnostic Man: The Doctrine of Basilides," in Joseph Campbell, ed., *The Mystic Vision: Papers from the Eranos Yearbooks*, (London: Routledge, 1969), 210-246; and Edward Conze, "Buddhism and Gnosis," in *Further Buddhist Studies*, (London: Luzac, 1975), 15-32. Quispel rejects the influence of Buddhism on Basilides, but Conze does not, on comparative grounds.
11 Hippolytus, *Refutation of All Heresies*, VII.ix
12 Ibid.
13 Hippolytus, *Ref.*, VII.x.

14 Ibid., VII.x, xiv.

15 Ibid., VII.xiv.

16 See Clement of Alexandria, *Strom*.II.20

17 See Clement of Alexandria, *Strom*. IV.12

18 Hippolytus, *Ref*. VII.ix

19 See note 3, above, and in particular, Quispel, 225-226 on Basilides and Platonism. Gnosticism, Hermetism, and Platonism, but particularly Gnosticism and Platonism shared an emphasis on the transcendence of dualism. This tradition, which Damascius certainly represented, was what confessional Christianity relegated to the margins, with very negative consequences.

20 Clement of Alexandria, *Strom*. IV.12

21 Quispel claims that "this God whom Basilides encountered in his most secret heart is the Gnostic God, a nothingness beyond thought and will, unconscious, and containing within it the future universe in a state of unconsciousness(245)." There is a problem with the wording here, in that "transcendence of transcendence" is not unconsciousness—it is, rather, the transcendence of dualistic consciousness. This is an important distinction.

22 Quispel, op. cit., 246.

23 Deuteronomy 7:1-5. This passage helps explain why European settlers in the Americas mostly desecrated or ignored Native American sacred sites and understanding of sacred nature. The settlers, carrying their Bibles, were carrying on this Deuteronomic tradition of destroying the sacred stones and poles of the indigenous peoples of the land that they were appropriating.

24 Deuteronomy 20:10-18

25 Psalms 137: 7-9.

26 I Samuel 15:3.

27 See Regina Schwartz, *The Curse of Cain: The Violent Legacy of Monotheism*, (Chicago: U of Chicago P, 1997), p. 17.

28 It is quite interesting that the same ethos was consciously and unconsciously continued in Mormonism. When in 2007-2008, Mitt Romney was a candidate for the United States presidency, the following kind of remark was not unusual: "'There's a member of the tribe that's up there,' Nathan Oman, an assistant professor at William and Mary School of Law, said last month [January, 2008], adding that he had not yet decided whom to vote for. 'What happens to him is a test of whether or not our tribe gets included in the

political universe.'" From Suzanne Sataline, "Mormons Dismayed by Harsh Spotlight," *The Wall Street Journal*, 8 February 2008, p. A12. [A1, A12].

29 See Arthur Versluis, *Magic and Mysticism: An Introduction to Western Esotericism*, (Lanham: Rowman, 2007). By way of contrast, see *The New Inquisitions*, (New York: Oxford UP, 2006), which is a survey of exoterist inquisitionalism on the putative Left and Right.

30 See Jean Baudrillard, C. Turner, trs., *The Intelligence of Evil*, (Oxford: Berg, 2005), p. 91.

31 Ibid., p. 90.

32 See Baudrillard, op. cit., pp. 128-129.

33 Quoted in David Biele, *Gershom Scholem: Kabbalah and Counter-history*, (Cambridge: Harvard UP, 1979), p. 11.

34 Ibid., p. 75, quoting Scholem's 1937 letter to Zalman Schocken entitled "A Candid Word About the True Motives of My Kabbalistic Studies."

35 See Peter Sloterdijk, "Der mystiche Imperativ," in *Mystische Zeugnisse aller Zeiten und Völker*, (München: Diederichs, 1993), 9-44. See also Sloterdijk, *Eurotaoismus*, (Frankfurth: Suhrkamp, 1996) and *Weltfremdheit* (Frankfurt: Suhkamp, 1993), the latter unfortunately based on the usual misconstructions of Gnosticism.

36 See the work of Stephen Katz on how "mysticism" is a "construct."

37 See, for example, John Lukacs, *A New Republic*, (New Haven: Yale UP, 2004 ed.), particularly the final section on the Bush, Jr. administration. See also George Carey, "The Future of Conservatism," *Modern Age*, 47(2005)4: 291-300, and Arthur Versluis, "The Revolutionary Conservatism of Jefferson's Small Republics," *Modern Age* 48(2006)1: 1-12.

38 Plotinus, *Enneads* III.viii.8

39 Plotinus, *Enneads* III.viii.6

40 Famously, the Gnostics recognized that some people are by nature "hylic," that is to say, are infatuated with and unable to recognize anything beyond the material or physical-temporal world. Others are "psychic," that is, live primarily in an intermediate realm of the psyche, perhaps akin to what today we might term psychology, and only a comparative few are "pneumatic," that is to say, are drawn to gnosis, or direct individual realization of the *pneuma* or spirit.

41 See Arthur Versluis, *Wisdom's Children*, (Albany: SUNY, 1999); see also Versluis, "The Mystery of Böhme's Ungrund," *Studies in*

Spirituality (11(2001): 205-211. The one figure in whose work the negative theology of *Ungrund* and *Nichts* did become central was John Pordage (1610-1681). See Versluis, *The Wisdom of John Pordage*, (St. Paul: New Grail, 2003).

42 See Jacob Böhme, *Epistles*, II.24, II.36, II.43, II. 46.

43 See Böhme, *Epistles*, 11.1 ff.

44 Ibid., 11.24.

45 Ibid., 13.11

46 See Dionysius, *Divine Names*, 589B

47 I refer to Western Christianity because it is in Roman Catholicism that the Inquisition took on its most developed institutional form, but also because the inquisitional pathology moved out of Western religion into the secular millennialist totalitarian dictatorships of the twentieth century, as documented in *The New Inquisitions*. The inquisitional pathology is of course in itself a human, not a Christian tendency, but we can see it appearing with special intensity in Christian history.

48 See Bernadette Roberts, *The Path to No-Self* (Albany: SUNY, 1991), *The Experience of No-Self* (Boston: Shambhala, 1982), and *What is Self?* (Austin: M. B. Goens, 1989).

49 See Roberts, *The Experience of No-Self: A Contemplative Journey*, (Albany: SUNY, 1993), p. 128.

50 Bernadette Roberts, *The Path to No-Self: Life at the Center*, (Albany: SUNY, 1991), p. xv

51 Ibid., p. 199. After acknowledging Eckhart as an antecedent figure for her, Roberts then holds that "he is unique and unlike any other Christian mystic (p. 203)." This is true, but begs the question of whether he nonetheless himself belongs to a larger current in the Christian tradition, that of the via negativa, to which Roberts herself also belongs.

52 I am using the word "gnostic" here because it is arguably more precise than "mystic," which is associated with visionary experiences and much else that is at best ancillary to the experience of gnosis, that is, of inner spiritual illumination and transcendence of the self-other dualism that characterizes conventional or usual modes of human consciousness. Practically speaking, for our purposes here, "gnostic" and "mystic" are synonymous, and refer to those who have experienced gnosis in the via negativa tradition.

53 Roberts, *The Experience of No-Self*, op. cit., p. 9

54 Ibid., p. 25

55 *Experience*, p. 37

56 Ibid., p. 60.

57 Ibid., p. 63.

58 *Path to No-Self*, p. 124.

59 Ibid., p. 146,

60 *Experience*, pp. 161-162

61 Ibid., p. 108

62 Both Emerson in *Nature* and Thoreau in *Walden* offered spiritual narratives (like Emerson's "transparent eyeball" passage) that are more directly personal accounts of individual mystical experience than what we find in the works of Meister Eckhart.

63 See, in this regard, Arthur Versluis "Eric Voegelin, Antignosticism, and the Origins of Totalitarianism," *Telos* 124 (Summer 2002/3): 173-182, and the equivalent chapter in *The New Inquisitions* (New York: Oxford UP, 2006).

64 Ibid., p. 79

65 See Keiji Nishitani, *Religion and Nothingness*, (Berkeley: U of California P, 1982).

66 Ibid., 225.

67 See Pordage's description in *Sophia*, in Arthur Versluis, ed., *Wisdom's Book: The Sophia Anthology*, (St. Paul: Paragon House, 2000).

68 See *The Wisdom of John Pordage* (St. Paul: New Grail, 2003), p. 55.

69 Plotinus, *Enneads*, III.viii.10

70 See Carl Schmitt, "The Visibility of the Church," in *Roman Catholicism and Political Form*, Gary Ulmen, trs., (Westport: Greenwood, 1996), p. 52. [*Römischer Katholizismus und politische Form*, (München: Theatiner-Verlag, 1925)]

71 See Carl Schmitt, *The Nomos of the Earth in the International Law of the* Jus Publicum Europaeum, Gary Ulmen, trs., (New York: Telos, 2003), pp. 59-60.

72 Carl Schmitt, G. Schwab, trs., *The Concept of the Political*, (New Brunswick: Rutgers, 1976), p. 60. [*Der Begriff des Politischen*, (München: Duncker & Humblot, 1932)]

73 Robertson, Alexander, and J. Donaldson, eds., *Ante-Nicene Fathers*, (Edinburgh: T & T Clark, 1989 ed.) III. 643. See Tertullian's treatise "Scorpiace," op. cit., III.633-648.

74 *The Concept of the Political*, p. 64.

75 Ibid., p. 67.

76 Ibid., p. 65.

77 For an extensive historical survey, see Arthur Versluis, *Magic and Mysticism: An Introduction to Western Esotericism*, (Lanham: Rowman & Littlefield, 2007). Some scholars of esotericism, notably Antoine Faivre, have argued in effect that esotericism begins in the early modern period, around 1600. See Antoine Faivre, *Access to Western Esotericism*, (Albany: SUNY, 1993).

78 Carl Schmitt, *The Leviathan in the State Theory of Thomas Hobbes*, G. Schwab, trs., (Westport: Greenwood, 1996), p. 29.

79 Ibid., p. 60.

80 Ibid., p. 62.

81 These are themes and figures discussed at length in Arthur Versluis, *The New Inquisitions: Heretic-hunting and the Intellectual Origins of Modern Totalitarianism*, (New York: Oxford UP, 2006).

82 See Gary Ulmen, "Introduction," in Carl Schmitt, *Roman Catholicism and Political Form*, op. cit., xv, citing Schmitt, *Glossarium: Aufzeichnungen der Jahre 1947-1951*, Eberhard Freiherr von Medem, ed, (Berlin: Duncker & Humblot, 1991), [23 May 1949], 243.

83 See Richard Wolin, *The Frankfurt School Revisited*, (New York: Routledge, 2006), 243-252. For my discussion of Schmittianism, see *The New Inquisitions*, 49-59.

84 See Johannes Althusius, *Politica*, Frederick Carney, trs., (Indianapolis: Liberty Fund, 1995), (IX.21-23), 72-73.

85 See Arthur Versluis, "Voegelin's Anti-gnosticism and the Origins of Totalitarianism," *Telos*, 124 (Summer 2002): 173-182.

86 See Hans Blumenberg, *The Legitimacy of the Modern Age* Robert Wallace, trs., (Cambridge: MIT, 1983), pp. 125 ff.

87 Ibid., p. 126.

88 Ibid., p. 137.

89 See on this point Versluis, *Wisdom's Children: A Christian Esoteric Tradition*, (Albany: SUNY P, 1999).

90 See Lynn White, "The Historical Origins of Our Environmental Crisis," *Science* 156 (1967):1203-1207.

91 See, for instance, Fredric Jameson, "Periodizing the 60s," in Sohnya Sayres, et al., eds., *The 60s Without Apology*, (Minneapolis: University of Minnesota Press, 1984), 178-209, which concludes by discoursing on the "therapeutic" aspects of the Chinese "cultural revolution," implying that Mao just didn't go far enough, and by asserting that the "sense of freedom and possibility" of the 1960s was merely an

historical illusion, while the 1980s will surely be characterized by the "extension of class struggle" [the only authentic reality, which is dualistic] "into the furthest reaches of the globe (208-209)."

92 Jeff Nuttal, "Applications of Extasy," in Joseph Berke, ed., *Counter Culture*, (London: Peter Owen, 1969), 208.

93 Allen Ginsberg, "Consciousness and Practical Action, in Berke, ed., *Counter Culture*, 172.

94 Ginsberg, in Berke, ed., 173.

95 Ibid., 180.

96 Ibid., 176.

97 Although the term "counter-culture" is fundamentally misleading, I continue to use it here because it is still in general use and because I do not see an appropriate alternative to it.

98 See Arthur Versluis, *Magic and Mysticism*, (Lanham, MD: Rowman, 2007), for a discussion of these primary terms and currents within Western history.

99 This notion still impels discourse on the putative Left, and helps also to explain the continuing attraction that Stalin or Mao holds for some. The motive impulse behind such discourse was captured by Dostoevsky in *The Brothers Karamazov*, in his figure of the Grand Inquisitor. See Arthur Versluis, *The New Inquisitions*, (New York: Oxford University Press, 2006), 10-11, 136-137.

100 Analogously, one might expect a renegade band or bands of evangelical Christians to attempt to "speed the coming of the millennium"—if not for the belief that the timing of such things in the end belongs to God, not man. The Weatherman group acknowledged no divine constraints on humanity—everything is up to us, they believed.

101 Hence after the communes were established came the anthropologists, who studied the new natives in their habitats.

102 Jacques Ellul, *The Technological Society*, John Wilkinson, trs., (New York: Knopf, 1964); Herbert Marcuse, *One-Dimensional Man* (Boston: Beacon, 1964); and Lewis Mumford, *The Myth of the Machine*, (New York: Harcourt, 1967).

103 See Theodore Roszak, *The Making of a Counter Culture*, (Berkeley: U of California Press, 1995), 263-264.

104 Roszak, 265. It is worth noting that Carlos Casteneda's *The Teachings of Don Juan* was published in 1968.

105 Ralph Waldo Emerson, *Nature*, (Boston: Munroe, 1836), 90.

106 See, on Emerson and Asian traditions, Arthur Versluis, *American*

Transcendentalism and Asian Religions, (New York: Oxford University Press, 1993). Emerson's immediatism is one reason that his Harvard Divinity School Address was seen as so scandalous. For an exceptionally clear example of countercultural Emersonesque gnosticism, see Stephen [Gaskin], *The Caravan*, (New York: Harper, 1972).

107 See Hans Blumenberg, *The Legitimacy of the Modern Age*, Robert Wallace, trs., (Cambridge, MA: MIT Press, 1983), 137. See also Arthur Versluis, "Antignosticism and the Origins of Totalitarianism," *Telos* 124(2003): 173-182, and Versluis, *The New Inquisitions*, op. cit., 69-84.

108 It is worth remarking in a note on Traditionalism, although the topic would be tangential in the main text. Traditionalism of the Guénon/Schuon line, as a set of essentially anti-modern doctrines, is fundamentally a modern phenomenon, but whereas modernism looks forward and emphasizes progress, Traditionalism looks backward and rejects progress. Hence Traditionalism shares more than a little in common with the culture wars in the American academy mentioned earlier, not least the inclination to valorize the past over the present and future. Traditionalism is an intellectual, distinctly modern narrative of decline, and as such tends to foreclose the possibility of new cultures; it emphasizes instead a posited primordial culture of great antiquity, an idealized Sufic Islam, or perhaps an idealized medieval Catholicism. All the same, Traditionalism recognizes the vertical dimensions of the sacred, which secular modernism, broadly speaking, does not.

109 Such assumptions are characteristic of both Right and Left in modernity. This is why, incidentally, Nazi legal theorist Carl Schmitt was so widely embraced not only by those belonging to the state-centralist Right, but also by many on the Left. The well-known journal *Telos* led the way in this regard, publishing a seemingly endless series of articles and issues devoted to Schmitt and to Schmittian theorism, but there were many others on the so-called Left who also jumped on this bandwagon. Schmitt's politico-theological dualism explicitly derives from Judeo-Christian exoteric dualism, and is congenial to modern political theorists whose premises are also dualistic and emerge from a Hobbesian embrace of the Leviathan/Behemoth/centralized/totalized state.

110 I discussed this tendency at great length in *The New Inquisitions*,

(New York: Oxford UP, 2006).

111 The term "contemplation" is a curious one. Its root is the same as "time," or "temporality," and as a result, it carries the residue of time along with it—or to put it another way, "contemplation" and its cognates proceed from and in some respects belong to time. "Noesis" does not carry these or similar associations.

112 One has to note that few countries in the world are more technologically inclined than modern Switzerland. In such respects—technological emphasis, financial complexity, lack of humanities or culture—Switzerland is not necessarily an ideal model. But nonetheless, it retained just those characteristics mentioned, and in particular, its confederational and neutral character, as well as its localism, more than any other country in Europe, certainly more than the imperial United States. In fact, these two countries make an instructive contrast, since their constitutions and original values actually were quite similar at their inception.

CPSIA information can be obtained at www.ICGtesting.com
Printed in the USA
LVOW06s1924150514

385955LV00001B/146/P

Index